The Seeds

of the Prairie

A Story of Three Immigrant Families

By

Fauneil Fremont

i

ISBN: 978-1-965951-26-2 (sc)

Seraphim Global Media LLC

155 Willowbrook Blvd Ste 110 Wayne, NJ 07470

+1 888-347-1877

fullfillment@seraphimgml.com

Table of Contents

Preface

The story is about three Prussian families who emigrate to the United States: the Bechs, the Meritzes, and the Getzmers. The Bechs traveled by wagon train to Nebraska in 1877, followed by the Meritzes in 1891. By 1895, when the Getzmers moved to Nebraska, there was no more land available to homestead. They started farming as renters. Later, they were able to purchase land.

The main part of the story begins in 1912, when Lisetta Meritz is born, and it ends in 1938, during the Great Depression. Lisetta, the author's mother, died in 2013. Prior to her death, Fauneil recorded data she had gathered about Lisetta's life: the history of her family and descriptions of day-to-day living on a farm.

Fauneil also found information from cemeteries, schools, the Norfolk Public Library, and the archives of St. Paul's Lutheran Church. Thus, the book became a biographical human-interest tale and a history of the Hoskins, Winside, and Norfolk areas of northeastern Nebraska.

Fauneil changed the last names of family members and their acquaintances. Their first names remain the same. Although she created the dialogue from imagination, she attuned it to her mother's remembrances of the characters.

A quote from Fauneil: "I never met my grandfather Gus, but through my mother, he became alive. I am grateful for the many hours she spent with me in describing life from 1912-1938 and the memories that had been relayed to her by her mother, Minnie."

Part I: The Bechs, the Meritzes, and the Getzmers

Chapter 1: New Life

It's a beautiful day for the baptism, Minnie thought as she looked out the window. It was October. Fall had arrived. For this occasion of "new life," the countryside was ironically displaying signs that summer was dying and winter approaching. The dried grass complemented the golden stalks in the harvested cornfields and in the brown earth where the cattle had trampled the stubble in the oat fields.

The trees had put on their best attire for the occasion and stood proudly waiting for the Bechs to arrive. There were the spruce and the pines that had been planted as windbreaks to the fields and the buildings. The hundred-foot spruce stood with horizontal branches covered with stiff deep-green needles. The forty-foot pines were not as grand as the spruce, but their needles were equally as stiff, and their brown cones just as hard. They, too, were ready for the cold and wind of winter.

The stark appearance of the windbreaks was enlivened with the striking beauty of the poplars and the cottonwoods. Some of the poplars had grown as tall as the spruce. Their columnar, upward-spreading branches were covered with triangular, golden-yellow leaves. The cottonwoods were as tall as the pines but were much broader. Their coarsely toothed, bright lemon-colored leaves would be the last to fall this season.

The countryside was dotted with the colors of the maples, locusts, and ash trees that had been planted here and there – in a pasture, along a lane, next to a barn. Now that the leaves of the maples had turned red-orange, the green, silvery-striped barks were even more beautiful than they had been in the summer. The locusts were loaded with yellow oval leaflets, ready to drop any minute from the arching branches to which they clung. The squarish branches of the ash trees displayed purplish leaves – leaves that said, "The advent season is near."

Minnie heard Lisetta cry. Her nap time was over. Minnie went to the bedroom to feed and change Lisetta and to dress her in the baptismal gown. It was the same gown that her brother Lyle had worn three years ago; and, not only Lyle, but all of the babies in the Bech family since Minnie could remember.

The long, white cotton gown was trimmed with hand-made lace. Minnie had washed, starched, and ironed the gown this summer. She wondered if the stiffness of the gown would bother Lisetta, but she seemed perfectly content after Minnie had dressed her and put her back down in the buggy.

Minnie called to Lyle to come and help her. "I want you to wheel the buggy back and forth until the Bechs arrive," she said. Not long after, Minnie heard the sound of horses' hooves. She picked up Lisetta, called to her husband Gus, and went out to greet the first arrivals – Reverend

John Dowidat, who would perform the ceremony, and his wife Anna, Minnie's half-sister. The next to arrive were Minnie's sister Ella, who had married Gus's brother Ed, and their daughters Loretta and Engeline. The rest of the family all seemed to arrive at once even though they had come in different carriages.

Minnie waited until all of the greetings had been exchanged and everyone had had a good look at the baby. Then she and her husband ushered all of the guests into the parlor, where they formed two circles around the "baptismal font." Reverend Dowidat began the ceremony by invoking the name of the Trinity. Turning to Gus, he said, "Name this child."

"Lisetta Augusta Meritz," answered Gus.

At the end of the ceremony, Reverend Dowidat made a sign of the cross over her head and said, "Lisetta, you have been chosen as God's child. May the Lord bless you and keep you, and may your life be filled with the knowledge and love of God. Amen."

"Amen. Let's eat!" said Gus.

As Gus led the guests into the dining room, Minnie carried Lisetta back to her buggy. Lisetta had fallen asleep somewhere between the opening invocation and the prayer of blessing. When Minnie returned, the adults were already seated at the dining room table, and the children were waiting patiently around the table in the kitchen. Minnie had not set a place for herself. She would serve the others and eat afterwards, as a good hostess should. Following grace by the reverend, Minnie started the homemade bread and butter around the table and then went into the kitchen to dish up the bowls of Schwarzsauer.

The conversation at the table consisted of the food, weather, crops, cattle, and the price of land. If they had lived in the city, the election of 1912, with Wilson versus Roosevelt, might well have dominated their conversation. But, here in the country, their world was a small, local one.

At one point, Gus attempted to divert the conversation to automobiles. On his trips to Norfolk to sell cattle or to purchase farm supplies, he had been seeing automobiles more and more frequently on the streets. Gus wanted an automobile, but he also wanted the approval of Minnie's father.

"What would you think, Herr Bech," he asked, "if Minnie and I purchased an automobile?"

"Ach, save your money!" exclaimed August Bech. "If you want to spend your money, buy some more land." This had been August Bech's motto from his early days as a pioneer. He had started out with an eighty-acre homestead, and by the time he and Augusta had retired and moved into Hoskins, they owned close to two thousand acres of land. "If you want to be somebody, get yourself an expensive buggy and a snazzy team of horses." August Bech was really referring to himself. When he had lived on the farm, he always rode in style whenever he went visiting. He had his hired men polish his black buggy until it looked like black marble, and before they hitched up his white team, they had spent hours currying and grooming the horses and dressing them in their expensive harnesses. And before August Bech stepped into his buggy from his front porch, he had had plenty of attention paid to himself. His black suit was pressed and completely devoid of lint, his shoes shone like mirrors, and he clenched a long, expensive cigar between his teeth.

Well, thought Gus, *you had your black buggy and your snazzy team, but times are changing, and I'm going to have a snazzy automobile one of these days.*

*   *   *

Minnie found little time to play with her growing children. She was too busy milking the cows, hoeing the garden, gathering the eggs, helping in the fields, cooking, baking, canning, cleaning, washing, ironing, mending, embroidering. But she kept her children close. As she worked, she gave Lyle little tasks to do to teach him the value of work. Lisetta was too young to help yet, but Minnie gave her things to play with that would later become tools of work: cobs, clothespins, lids, kettles, spoons.

Unlike Minnie, Gus always found time for relaxation. After supper he enjoyed smoking his cigar on the porch, visiting with Lyle, or rocking Lisetta in his rocking chair. In the daytime, Gus often turned work into play by taking Lyle and Lisetta with him when he inspected his fields. On these occasions, he rode Beauty, one of the tamer horses. He held Lisetta ahead of him in the saddle while Lyle hung on behind.

During the harvest season, Lyle and Lisetta especially enjoyed watching Hank Getzmer, one of the farm workers, pick corn. Hank enjoyed putting on a performance for them. To impress them, he picked the corn as fast as lightning. A horse and wagon traveled alongside him as he walked next to a row of corn. Without taking his eyes off the corn, Hank yanked an ear of corn with his right hand, another with his left, threw each over his shoulder into the wagon and reached for the next ears. The horse knew just what to do. When she heard the ears hit the baseboard of the wagon, she moved a few feet forward and waited for the next kerplunks. As she moved, she grabbed a tasty green shuck of corn for munching.

Life for the Meritz family was centered around the farm during the week; on Sundays, it centered around church, family, and friends. Every Sunday Minnie, Gus, Lyle, and Lisetta dressed in their Sunday clothes and headed for church in Hoskins, the village nearest to them. They left early enough to enjoy a leisurely drive. In the spring, they enjoyed the brown fields turning to green as the young sprouts peeped through the earth. In the summer, they enjoyed the sweet smell of newly-cut hay, the oats rolling in the breeze, and the cornstalks climbing higher and higher each week. In the fall, they enjoyed the brightly colored trees and the cattle grazing in the harvested fields. In the winter, Gus hitched the team to the sleigh instead of the buggy. Lisetta and Lyle huddled together under thick quilts and enjoyed listening to the rhythmic tinkling of the bells on the horses' harnesses.

3

Trinity Evangelical Lutheran Church in Hoskins was a wooden church with a bell tower atop its shingle roof. Four front steps led up to double doors, which opened into a narrow vestibule. On the walls of the vestibule were rows of pegs, where parishioners could hang their coats and mufflers.

As the worshippers entered the sanctuary, they were greeted by the altar picture of the "Ascension of Christ," which stood out against the white-painted, ornately carved wood of the altar. Two brass chandeliers hung from the blue-painted metal ceiling. The walls of the sanctuary were painted alabaster, and the tall arched windows were of colored glass.

What the sanctuary possessed in beauty, it lacked in comfort. An aisle separated rows of unupholstered hard wooden pews, which were bolted to a bare wooden floor. Wood was everywhere: To the right of the wooden altar was a wooden lectern; to the left a wooden pulpit with wooden steps leading up to it; to the left of the pulpit was a wooden hymn board, where hymn numbers were posted. Because of all of this wood, the sanctuary was acoustically "alive." Pastor Aaron could have preached softly and still have been heard, but his goal was to keep his parishioners from falling asleep during his long sermons.

Minnie and Gus both realized that the length and the wording of the service were not designed for children. However, they felt that "seeds" of faith could be planted. At two years of age, Lisetta's sole interest in the service was the organ playing. A walnut reed organ sat near the front of the sanctuary, off to one side. The organist worked the bellows of the organ by pumping the two pedals up and down with her feet while playing the hymn on the keyboard. Lisetta was fascinated with this obvious dexterity. Whenever a hymn began, her eyes darted to the organ.

Lyle was old enough to listen for a while to the sermon. When he grew tired of it, he consoled himself by thinking about what was in store for him after the service. Sunday afternoon was a time for fun, a time to visit relatives or neighbors.

*   *   *

On the first Thursday in July of 1914, Minnie and Gus dressed in their Sunday clothes. Minnie put on her black dress and her gold beads. Gus dressed in his black suit, a starched white shirt, and a black tie.

"Is it Sunday?" Lyle asked.

"No, it's Thursday."

"Why are we going to church on Thursday?"

"Today is Grandpa Bech's funeral. Remember, I told you that Grandpa Bech died on Monday."

Lyle and Lisetta whispered together during the buggy ride to Hoskins. They had not attended a funeral and did not understand the meaning of "death."   Lisetta had a better understanding when she saw Grandpa Bech lying in his coffin in the church. His eyes were closed, and he wasn't speaking or moving or smoking his cigar. At the end of the service, Lyle and Lisetta watched as Grandpa Bech's coffin was closed and then carried out of the church and into a buggy. Later they saw it taken out of the buggy, carried up a hill, and placed on a big stone slab in a building with a gate.

"What did you think of the mausoleum?" Minnie asked Gus on the way home.

"Pretty fancy! All that brick and tile and wrought iron sitting there in the middle of those other graves. I'd rather be buried in the ground."

*   *   *

A year and a half later, Lisetta almost joined her dead grandfather. Gus and Minnie were having a new house built on their farm. The Miller brothers from Norfolk, a city 15 miles from Hoskins, had been hired to build it. The house was to have a large front porch, a gracious entry hall with stairs leading to the second story; to the left of the hall would be a large living room and dining room; to the right a den; a kitchen in the rear; upstairs, four bedrooms and a bathroom.

Lisetta slipped out from noon dinner which Minnie had provided for the Millers and went in search of her new bedroom. The house was still in the open stage. The foundation had been laid, the rooms had been mapped out, and the frame was up. Wooden stairs led to the second story. Halfway up the stairs was an open landing. Lisetta climbed to the landing and then to the top of the stairs, but she didn't see anything that looked like a room. Climbing up had been easy, but finding her way back down was more difficult. At first, she maneuvered the steps, feeling for each one with her shoe. But when she got to the open landing, she was turned around. The steps headed a different direction. At the landing, Lisetta inched her way along and gingerly put out one foot for the next step. It wasn't there! She stretched her leg a little more to find it. And a little more. Ooooh, she knew she was falling – she felt a thud to her head – and then blackness.

When the Miller brothers went back to work, they found Lisetta in the basement. The child looked lifeless. They ran for Minnie, who sent Lyle for Gus. Minnie picked up Lisetta and cradled her in her arms as Gus hitched the team to the buggy. He put Lyle, Minnie and Lisetta in and headed for Hoskins to see Doctor Scheng.

The journey seemed endless: down the lane to the main road, up the hill, down the next, and the next and the next, cornfields on the right, oats on the left, an alfalfa pasture, prairie grass, a row of cottonwood trees, around a bend, another bend, a farmhouse, a herd of cattle, a grove of ash trees, a row of buildings – at last, Hoskins! - past the granary, the blacksmith, the hotel, the bank, the milliner, the post office, the grocery, the butcher, the doctor. "Whoa!" shouted Gus, pulling on the reins.

Lisetta was still unconscious. Doctor Scheng examined her carefully: head, spine, neck, torso, hips, legs, feet, arms, hands. "No broken bones," he said. He looked into her ears and her eyes. "No bleeding." He put ammonia under her nose. She coughed, opened her eyes, and looked around, dazed.

"Watch her for concussion," he advised. "Keep her quiet, but don't let her go to sleep today or tonight. "

"Danke Gott!" said Gus. "What good is a new house if your heart is empty."

Chapter 2: Young Lisetta

When Grandpa Bech died, the Bech estate was divided among August Bech's nine children – three from his wife Augusta's first husband, Matthius Escher, and six from August. Gus and Minnie were talking about the estate one evening at the supper table.

"Ella got two hundred forty acres, like I did," said Minnie, "but her land is better farmland; so that's why I got the three thousand cash."

"And Lisetta and Martha?" asked Gus.

"They inherited a farm together and the house in Hoskins."

The one hundred sixty acres of Minnie's across the road was currently being farmed by Hank. He had moved into the old house on the farm and was "batching" for himself. Minnie liked Hank. To show her admiration, she often baked bread, cookies, and coffee cake for him. She placed the baked goods in a basket, along with a jar of preserves, or some freshly-picked fruits and vegetables. Minnie gave Lisetta, who was four years old, the task of walking across the lane to deliver the basket to Hank.

Lisetta enjoyed this mission. It was not far to go – up their lane, a few yards along the road, and down the lane to Hank's. She especially liked going past the prairie meadow. This morning, she took in long, deep breaths of the sweet-smelling air. It was the purple and white clover that smelled so sweet. She went off the lane to pick a piece of white clover and held it up to her nose. Her footsteps startled a rabbit, who went scurrying through the grass. She spotted a bird's nest in the grass nearby. In the nest were four spotted eggs. Lisetta knew that she shouldn't touch the eggs because the mother bird wouldn't like it and would not come back to her nest. A few yards farther along, she heard the familiar warbling song of a meadow lark and caught sight of a brown bird with a yellow breast, a black bib, and white tail feathers.

When Lisetta reached the area where Hank was working, it was about nine o'clock. Hank had been toiling since five that morning. He saw Lisetta coming down the lane with her basket and set out to meet her.

"Guten Tag, Zettie!" Hank picked her up with her basket, lifted her high in the air, and set her down in one graceful swoop. "Let's sit here and have some Kaffeekuchen," he said as he spread his jacket on the meadow grass at the side of the lane. Lisetta loved her visits with Hank. He thought she was old enough to talk to, unlike some of the adults she knew. Usually, they talked about the Getzmer family, but this morning they talked about the prairie meadow. Lisetta had told Hank about picking the clover and seeing a meadow lark's nest, and Hank took this opportunity to point out some of the prairie vegetation to her. He picked a runner from a vine carrying orange trumpet-shaped flowers and held it up to her nose.

"This is honeysuckle. Smells as sweet as clover, huh?"

Lisetta sniffed it and nodded. Hank spread the tall grass with his fingers and picked a tiny plant growing close to the ground. It had oval leaves and dainty blue flowers in clusters.

"This is blue phlox." He gave it to Lisetta, who sniffed it and smiled. Hank spread the tall grass again and brought up some heart-shaped leaves with runners and tiny, deep-purple flowers.

"These are violets. They smell just like perfume. This is my favorite," added Hank as he handed Lisetta a shooting star, a small, single pink flower on a leafless stem. "The stem just shoots up alone out of the plant, like a star shoots out of the sky." Hank picked another shooting star whose flower had turned to seeds.

"Watch," he said, blowing the seeds. "Some of these seeds will be carried away by the wind. And some have fallen here into the grass. They'll stay here all through the winter, safe and warm. And next spring, beautiful new stars will shoot up out of the earth." He picked up Lisetta and lifted her up again high in the air.

That evening at the supper table, Lisetta tried to tell Lyle what she had learned about flowers, but Lyle wasn't interested; so, she changed the subject to the Getzmer family.

"Did you know there are twelve children in Hank's family?"

"No, there aren't that many," countered Lyle.

"Yes, there are! There's Anna and Max and Marie and Bill and Hank and Paul and Emil."

"That's only seven!" Lyle had been counting.

"And then there's Dick and Minnie – but they call her Mabel – and Ferd and Walter. He's the youngest."

"That's only eleven!"

Lisetta wrinkled her forehead and tried to remember. "No, Robert is the youngest, but he died."

"Well, if he died, there's only eleven."

Lisetta thought a moment. "Well then," she said proudly, "there's only nine because Max and Marie died, too!"

Minnie and Gus had been listening to this conversation. Lisetta would be five in August, and they had been wondering whether to send her to school at the end of the summer. Minnie looked at Gus.

"I think she's ready," she said.

A week later, Minnie wasn't so sure. Once again it was time for Lisetta to deliver the basket of baked goods to Hank. It was a gloomy day. The sky was blanketed with high gray clouds, the kind that kept the sun from shining but produced no rain. Because the air was chilly, Lisetta was wearing a sweater over a cotton dress. Although the day was gloomy, Lisetta wasn't. She was on her way to see Hank! As she skipped along, she hummed a tune to herself. When she came to the prairie meadow, she saw a big blue jay perched on a high branch of an ash tree. Caw, caw! Caw, caw! The bird swooped down at her. She ducked her head but wasn't frightened because she had often seen blue jays swoop at cats. She knew the bird was only bluffing.

Ah, there it was again – that sweet smell of the clover! Lisetta inhaled a deep breath of the sweet air. Suddenly she felt a tickle inside her sweater. A clover bee had crawled inside, and when she reached back, it stung her sharply on her shoulder. Lisetta screamed, dropped her basket, and tore off down the lane for home.

Minnie saw her coming and ran to meet her. Lisetta threw herself into Minnie's arms and sobbed uncontrollably. "Was ist los?" asked Minnie, but Lisetta could only point to her shoulder. Minnie examined the wound and discovered the bite. When Lisetta's sobs had subsided, Minnie explained to her that she had only been stung by a little bee and that she should go back, pick up her basket, and take it to Hank. Lisetta refused.

"Zettie, you do as you're told!" Minie ordered her.

* * *

At the supper table, Gus said, "Well, Zettie, I understand that you got stung by a bee today."

Lisetta nodded gloomily in her chair.

"That was a good lesson," said Gus. "Life is full of stings."

* * *

Gus sat smoking his cigar on the porch after supper. Lisetta stood close by the rocking chair and watched as a bird flew to the maple tree and perched on a limb.

"Oh, look at the bird with the red wings!"

"That's a red-winged blackbird," Gus answered. "If your mother were out here, she would want me to get my gun and shoot it."

"Why?" asked Lisetta.

"Blackbirds eat the chokecherries off the chokecherry bushes. You know that red jelly you like so much? Your mother makes that out of chokecherries – that is, unless the blackbirds get them first."

"Aren't there enough chokecherries for the blackbirds and for us, too?"

9

Gus didn't answer. He had caught sight of a figure coming down the lane. *That looks like Herr Getzmer,* thought Gus.

Wilhelm Reinold Getzmer had been a frequent visitor this summer. Now that Hank was farming Minnie's land across the road, Wilhelm regularly came to visit his son and then took an after-supper stroll to see Gus. In spite of the difference in their ages, they had become good friends. Wilhelm found Gus feisty and amusing, and Gus found "Herr Getzmer," as he called him, interesting and knowledgeable. Although Gus was self-taught and prided himself on going to school for only several months when he was seven, he was eager to learn as much as he could in informal ways. Wilhelm Getzmer could not only read and write well in German, but he had had an adventuresome past.

In comparison with the Bechs and the Meritzes , the Getzmers were poor newcomers in the area. Wilhelm and Emilia had married in Prussia in 1889 and had immigrated to America with their two small daughters, Anna and Marie, in 1893. For two years, they had lived with Wilhelm's brother Herman and his family near Cleveland, where Wilhelm helped Herman to farm wheat on "the heights" in the summer. In the winter, Wilhelm drove a milk wagon. In the two years they had lived in Ohio, they had experienced the death of their second daughter, Marie, the birth and death of their first son, Max, and the birth of their second son, Wilhelm Herman.

Young Wilhelm (Bill) was a tiny baby when they set out in 1895 to make a home in Nebraska. They took the train as far as Sioux City, where the railroad lines stopped. There they purchased a team of horses and a wagon, a few pieces of furniture, and then bounced the remaining eighty miles over dirt roads to the farm they would be renting near Winside, Nebraska. The wagon journey took its toll on Emilia, who was pregnant again. When her baby Bill was only seven months old, she prematurely gave birth to Hank.

During their last visit, Mr. Getzmer had talked about all of this and about his life in Prussia. He and Emelia had both grown up on farms near Schwetz and had had similar experiences. Wilhelm's father had died when he was four, and Emelia's mother had died when she was four-and-a-half.

Both families had been poor tenant farmers to wealthy Junker landowners. But, as poor as they were, Mr. Getzmer had explained to Gus, they were better off than their ancestors had been. Wilhelm's father, Wilhelm August, had had to wait until he was forty to marry because his life had been so uncertain. In Prussia, Mr. Getzmer explained, the young tenant farmers had been at the mercy of the government. Whenever a military crisis arose, the tenant farmers were the first to be taken off the land and conscripted into the army. At seven-year intervals, a military grant came up for renewal by the Prussian Parliament. Each time, Bismarck cleverly maneuvered either a war or a threat of war so that the Prussian Parliament would renew the military grant, enabling the army to stay strong. The military crises seemed endless. There were conflicts over Schleswig-Holstein, Hanover, Hesse, Nassau, and Frankfurt am Main and threats of war with Austria, France, and Russia.

By the time he and Emelia had left Prussia in 1883, Bismarck had fallen from power; but his successor, Caprini, had managed to renew an army grant by invoking danger from Russia. The injustice to the tenant farmers was still there. Wilhelm had just finished a term in the army and had saved all of his army pay while Emelia had eked out an existence for herself and their two daughters on the farm. As soon as Wilhelm mustered out of the army, he and Emelia, like his brother Herman before him and millions of other Europeans, left their war-weary world for the promise of a better life in America.

Now as Gus saw Mr. Getzmer approaching, he compared his own background with that of his friend. Gus's parents had come to Nebraska in 1891, but they had had enough money to homestead. The Moritz family had been property owners in Budzig, Prussia. Gus remembered well the Moritz Delicatessen in Budzig, which was first owned and operated by his grandparents. He also remembered the visitors to the Meritz home and the long hours of discussion about the unfair distribution of taxation, with most of the wealthy upper class taking advantage of the lower classes. Not long after William II came to the throne, the Meritz family emigrated – first Gus's oldest brothers, and then the rest of the family. Gus had been seven at the time.

In spite of our experiences and age, Gus reflected, *we have a lot in common*. We both have Prussian blood in our veins; we speak German; we're farmers on an American prairie; and we both like to play Schafskopf. Gus rose to greet his visitor.

"Guten Abend, Herr Getzmer!"

"Guten Abend, Gus! Wie geht's?"

Their conversation continued in a mixture of German and English. Lisetta was accustomed to a language mixture between her parents, but Mr. Getzmer had a thick accent, and she had to listen very carefully to understand him.

"Wollen Sie denn Schafskopf spielen?" asked Gus.

"Nein. None of your tricks ziss evening." Wihlelm changed the subject. "Soon you can move into your new house."

"Jawohl! That house will be a big change from this one. There's a basement in it, with a toilet and sink down there and running water, and a bathroom upstairs with a toilet and a sink and a bathtub. No more going outside when duty calls or using the chamber pot at night." Wilhelm smiled. "There's a furnace with hot-air registers in every room, and there's a new stove in the kitchen and a telephone on the wall so Minnie can ring up the cows in the barn to find out if they're ready to be milked."

Gus winked at Lisetta, who had a puzzled look on her face.

"Vutt about ziss house, Gus?"

"Well, Herr Getzmer, I haven't decided."

"A big family could live in ziss house. Wie viele Schlafzimmer have you upstairs?"

"Come and see!" By now, Gus knew that this was more than a friendly conversation, but he couldn't imagine why Herr Getzmer would want to move his family here when they were already situated on a farm near Winside . However, he was prepared to bargain and invited Herr Getzmer into the house.

"Well, let's have a look at this old palace we're leaving," said Gus as he held the door open for Wilhelm and Lisetta. Wilhelm had seen the downstairs several times before, but Gus was in a mood for fun.

"Now, here we have the parlor. It's big enough for most families. And here, off the parlor, is a bedroom – big enough and cozy enough for two." Gus led Wilhelm back through the parlor and into the dining room. "Now this room is big enough for all of your boys and all of your neighbors."

"Ja, ja," answered Wilhelm, "und zeh Prussian army too."

"Let's sneak up on Minnie," whispered Gus as he stepped into the kitchen, tiptoed up to Minnie, and tapped her on the shoulder. Minnie flinched and turned around from the sink.

"Guten Abend, Herr Getzmer!"

"Minnie, Herr Getzmer would like to see your kitchen."

Minnie looked around the room and pointed out her shelves and cupboards, the hand pump, and the wrought-iron stove. Then she showed him a small pantry to the left of the kitchen, and to the right, a screened-in porch where she kept tubs, buckets, and brooms. A line of overshoes stood along one wall of the porch.

"No one comes into my kitchen with overshoes on," said Minnie.

Finally, she pointed to a fruit cellar which was a few feet from the outside screen door. She went back to the dishes as Gus led Wilhelm back through the kitchen and into the dining room again. Gus opened a door and motioned to Wilhelm to look inside.

"Another bedroom," Gus said.

Wilhelm was beginning to wonder if he would ever be shown the upstairs. Gus opened the door adjacent to the bedroom, bowed to the waist, and said pompously, "Mein lieber Herr, nach Ihnen." The wooden stairs were steep and narrow. Wilhelm climbed up slowly and carefully, with Gus teasing him from behind, "Schnell, schnell!"

"This is our hotel," Gus said. "Right now, we have six rooms, all unoccupied."

"Ja, it looks like a hotel," commented Wilhelm.

There were three bedrooms on either side of the hall; the door to each stood closed; the only thing missing was a number on each door.

"I can show you each of the bedrooms, but they're all identical. All of our hotel guests get treated alike."

Gus opened the door to the first bedroom on the right and allowed Wilhelm to enter first. After Gus and Lisetta were in, there wasn't much space left. The room was just big enough for a double bed, a night stand, a small bureau, and a side chair. Gus stepped past the bed and opened a door to a small walk-in closet.

"There's a closet like this in each bedroom," he said. Lisetta, who had been tagging along, hopped up on the bed as Wilhelm walked over to peek at the closet.

"You ready for bed, Zettie?" teased Gus.

"No!" She quickly hopped down and stepped out the door. She purposely did not look down the hall at all the closed doors. She remembered being up here playing one day with Lyle, who went from room to room making strange noises until she ran downstairs and outside into the sunshine.

"Here, hold my hand," Gus said to Lisetta as he led Wilhelm back downstairs and out onto the porch.

"Well, Herr Getzmer," Gus said, "I can sell you this hotel for three thousand."

"Ach, Gus, I just bought a farm fur drei tausend."

"A farm?"

"Ja, zeh Barkholz farm. Fur zwei und zwanzig Jahre, vee vorked hard and saved. It's too late fur Annie und Bill und Hank, but vee still have funf boys und Mabel zu Hause."

"One bedroom for each upstairs," said Gus.

"Ja. In Vinside, wir haben zwei kleine Hauser."

"You live in two houses at the same time? Unmoglich!"

Mr. Getzmer explained that when they had moved from Cleveland, there was only a four-room house on the farm they rented, with a small kitchen, a dining room, and two small bedrooms. At first, he and Emilie and the baby had slept in one bedroom, and the two young children had shared the other. Then another baby came, and another, and soon there were four children sleeping in a bedroom. Eventually they had needed sleeping room for ten children and had found it cheaper to build a second house a few yards away rather than to add on to the existing house. Since then, Mabel and all of the boys had been sleeping in one house and eating in the other. Gus shook his head in amazement and glanced at Lisetta to see if she had understood this story. Lisetta took this as an invitation to enter the conversation.

"There was an old woman who lived in a shoe. She had so many children, she didn't know what to do," she recited.

"She should have lived in two houses, nicht so, Zettie?" Gus turned to Wilhelm, "Well, this house is certainly big enough. But you would be three miles from your land. How would you look after your livestock?"

"Gus, vee vouldn't live here! Last veek I took ze train to Norfolk und talked mit Herr Stahlkup. He moves houses."

"Moves houses? How can he do that? Through the pastures? He takes down fences?

"Zeh whole house moves. Mit boards und rollers. You sell me zeh house fur ein hundert – you see it move."

"Well, Herr Getzmer, it would make me very happy to think of your family living under one roof, but I'll have to talk it over with Minnie. Give me a day to work it out."

"Schon gut. Es wird dunkel," said Wilhelm, looking at the sky. He tipped his hat, "Bis morgen."

As Gus and Lisetta watched Mr. Getzmer's figure getting smaller and smaller down the lane, Gus was dreaming about how he would spend the hundred dollars. On each of his recent visits to Norfolk, he had stopped by the Buick showrooms to look at the roadster in the window – black (Minnie would like that), four doors, leather seats, a glass windshield in front, a top, and Eisen-glass curtains to pull down when it rains. The price: one hundred and fifty dollars. *My cattle are about ready for market*, he figured. *If I sold them, I'd have more than enough for a "snazzy" black automobile.*

* * *

The house-moving operation started at the beginning of July. Gus watched as thick wooden beams were placed under the house to shore it up before the house was taken off its foundation. The porch was detached from the house. Then rollers were placed underneath the house and attached to the beams.

Emil, Dick, Ferd, and Walter Getzmer took down fences and then replaced them as the house was moved through the pastures. The house moved inch by inch. Mr. Stahlkup drove a team of white workhorses, which pulled the house over a series of planks. The Getzmer boys kept repositioning the planks as the rollers moved forward. Toward the end of the move, the thick planks had been worn almost as thin as toothpicks.

By the beginning of August, the house had been moved through Gus's pastures and across the road. Gus drove out one morning to see how the operation was going. The Getzmer boys were seated on the grass, eating their breakfast. Their sister Mabel was cooking in the kitchen and carrying items in and out to them.

"Good morning, Mr. Meritz!" she said. "Would you like something to eat?"

"No, thank you, Mabel. Are you cooking in that house?"

"Ja, the boys and I have been living here all during the move. The house moves so slowly, you hardly get bounced around inside." Gus shook his head in amazement.

"When do you expect to be relocated?" he asked Emil, who was the oldest.

"I figure another two weeks through the pasture, then about a week to put down a new foundation, and then another week to rebuild the porch."

"You're a spunky lot," said Gus as he tipped his hat and rode off.

*   *   *

By the end of the summer, the move was complete. The Getzmers were living in the Meritz's old house on their new farm, and Gus and Minnie had only a foundation where the old house had stood and were comfortably situated in their new house. The old Buick had been replaced by a new one. Gus had wasted no time. He left the buggy and the team in the barn more and more these days when he drove to Norfolk, Winside, Hoskins, Wayne, or Stanton.

 According to Minnie, he drove too much and too fast. Minnie rode with Gus if they were going together, but she had no desire to learn how to drive. Horses were good enough for her. And so, at the end of August, when it was time for Lyle and Lisetta to go to school, Minnie hitched up Beauty to a two-wheel cart (on a busy morning, it was faster to hitch a horse to a cart than a team to a buggy) and pulled up to the front porch.

"Lyle! Zettie! Macht schnell!" she yelled. Lyle came out first, dressed in a cotton shirt and overalls and sturdy shoes. After a few minutes, Lisetta crept out of the house.

"Come along, you slow poke!" Minnie was getting cross. As Lisetta climbed onto the cart, Minnie could see that her little girl was apprehensive.

"You look very nice," she said, consolingly.

Lisetta looked down at her clothing. She was wearing a colorful cotton dress, which had been heavily starched and ironed. Over the dress she wore a stiff, very white apron. Her legs were covered with long, black cotton stockings, and her high-top shoes were neat and clean. She felt her hair, which was drawn tightly back from her face and braided in one strand, which hung down her back.

Both Lyle and Lisetta carried black tin lunch boxes. "Don't open them now," ordered Minnie, "and at morning recess, only eat the Kaffeekuchen. Save the rest until noontime. And don't forget to bring them home when school is over." Minnie had even more orders when she drew up in front of the school to let them out. "Be quiet, obey your teacher, and show respect. Zettie, go to the outhouse at recess, but if you can't wait, be sure to let the teacher know. Lyle, look after your sister. Make sure she stays with you when you walk home. Lyle, you take Zettie in now!"

"Yes! Ma!" Lyle climbed down first and took Lisetta's lunch box while she climbed down. Lisetta swallowed hard as Minnie pulled away. Then she turned around and looked up at the building. It looked scary. The white-painted frame school sat on a hill near the intersection of two dirt roads. There were wooden steps leading up to double wooden doors. The front of the school was windowless. Lisetta jumped as a bell began to ring. She looked up and saw the bell swinging atop the steep shingle roof. "That means it's time for school," Lyle informed her.

As they stepped inside, Lisetta whispered, "Is this the school?"

"No, silly! This is the hall. Over here," he said, walking through a door, "is the boys' cloakroom. In the winter we hang our coats on these pegs and put our overshoes down here, like at church. We put our lunchboxes on these shelves up here." Lyle took Lisetta's lunchbox and set it next to his on a shelf. Over there (he pointed) is the girls' cloakroom."

Lyle led Lisetta from the hall through a door and into the classroom.

"Is this it?" whispered Lisetta.

"Yes," answered Lyle. "The pupils sit at these desks, two to a desk, and the teacher sits at her desk up there on the platform." Lyle pointed to the other end of the room. He led Lisetta up one of the aisles, past the big pot-bellied stove and between rows of wrought-iron desks with wooden tops. Miss Minerva Martin stood on the platform. As Lyle and Lisetta approached, she tapped on her desk with a ruler for attention.

"Good morning, class!" She did not introduce herself. Her students from last year knew her already, and the little ones would know her soon enough. "Let's begin with seat assignments."

Lisetta counted as Miss Martin called the names, twenty-four in all. Lisetta found herself seated next to Rose Lenser. In back of her was Walter Getzmer. She had seen him last summer when the house was being moved. As Lisetta turned around and looked at him shyly, Walter responded by gently pulling her pigtail.

Miss Martin tapped her desk again. "There will be no talking while school is in session," she warned, "unless I ask you to speak. Now, let's begin our work. You have much to learn this year. In the shelf under your desk top, you will find your books. The ridge at the top of the desk is the place to keep your pencil, your eraser, and your ink pen when you are not using them. The ink pen is to be used only if I ask you to use it, and it is not to be left in the inkwell."

Lisetta sat quietly as Miss Martin continued. "I have written here," she said as she pointed to a corner of the blackboard at the front of the room, "the times for each of the recitations. By the end of this week, I expect you to have these memorized. I will be erasing them because we need the entire blackboard for doing our arithmetic problems. As you see," she pointed, "we will begin with first and second grade reading at 9:15, then third and fourth at 9:30, fifth and sixth at 9:45, seventh and eighth at 10:00. Recess is at 10:15.   Following recess, we have spelling and grammar, then lunch. After lunch we have arithmetic and physiology, then recess, then geography and history. Remember to get these times memorized. When you come in next week, they will have been erased."

Lisetta was worried. Minnie had told her to obey her teacher, but how could she memorize what was on the board when she couldn't read? She looked over at Lyle across the room, but he was busy examining his pen. She looked around at Walter. "Don't worry," he whispered. "I'll help you."

Miss Martin looked at the big wall clock that hung above her desk. "It's time for first and second grade reading," she announced. "First and second graders, bring you books to the front. Older grades, you will find page numbers next to your recitation times. While I am busy with grades one and two, you are to read your assigned pages. I expect you all to be as busy as bees."

Chapter 3: The Princess

One of Gus's nicknames for Lisetta was "Nestkuchen." When winter came, the little "Nestkuchen" found it more difficult to get ready for school. No one fed the furnace at night, and until it was reloaded with wood and coal (which was Gus's job), the house was cold.

This morning when Minnie called her, Lisetta huddled for a while under her quilts. When Minnie called a second time, more insistently, Lisetta jumped out of bed and put on her clothes as fast as she could: first the long underwear, then the long, black cotton stockings over the underwear, then the slip, the flannel dress, the sweater, the apron, and the shoes.

Lisetta pulled up the window shade to see how much snow was on the ground, but the window was frosted over. She had heard the wind howling last night and the snow and ice driving against the window pane. But by this morning, the wind had abated.

"It's quiet out there," Minnie reported when she and Lyle came in from the milking. The snow is just sitting on the fence rails; there's no wind to blow it off."

"It looks like a foot of snow on the barn roof," added Lyle. "and there are icicles all along the east side of the roof."

After breakfast and the early morning chores, Minnie hitched Beauty to the sleigh and drove Lyle and Lisetta to school. When they arrived, Minnie told them that she would send Mabel Getzmer to fetch them in the afternoon.

"Oh, goody!" exclaimed Lisetta. Mabel, who was nine years older than Lisetta, sometimes did housework for Minnie for a small fee. Lisetta and Lyle enjoyed having Mabel around because she teased them, and they liked the attention. Lisetta went into the schoolhouse to tell Walter that his sister would be by to fetch them in the afternoon, but he wasn't there. Most of the other students were just arriving, bundled in their coats or jackets, galoshes, mufflers, mittens (one pair over another), ear muffs, and stocking caps. The cloakrooms were soon full of wraps and the cold dampness from the snow brought in on clothes and galoshes. The air inside the schoolroom was warm and steamy in comparison. It was cozy to be inside, working alongside schoolmates while the cold, white world outside waited for reading recitation to end and recess to begin.

At recess all of the boys and some of the girls went outside to build a snowman, or to slide downhill on a shovel or board or sled, or to engage in a snowball fight. Lisetta stayed inside. She had been in a snowball fight earlier in the winter and had suffered a headache for the rest of the day. Ralph Lundquist had been on the opposing team. Instead of making snowballs with his mittens on, he had taken them off and used the warmth of his hands to make ice balls out of the snow. One of these had caught Lisetta on the side of her head. Today at recess, Lisetta stayed inside and played tic-tac-toe on the blackboard with Rose. A few other girls drew pictures with their fingers on the frosted windows nearby.

"I wonder why Walter isn't in school today," Rose said, looking at Lisetta to see her reaction.

"I don't know, but I'll find out from his sister Mabel this afternoon. She's coming to fetch us after school."

Mabel was there promptly at four o'clock. "Hello, you big babies!" she greeted them as they climbed into the sleigh.

"We're not babies," retorted Lyle.

"Anyone who can't walk home from school in a little snow is a big baby. Why, I walked three miles in the snow today to get to your house, and when I got there, I washed and waxed all of the floors in the house. And when we get back, I have to help your mother with the supper."

"Will you be staying the night?" asked Lisetta.

"Yes, and tomorrow I'll drive you babies to school again."

"Mabel, why wasn't Walter in school today?" asked Lisetta.

"The strong winds last night blew down some trees and knocked down fences. Walt had to stay home to help. We don't have hired help on our farm like you pampered Meritzes." Lisetta did not know the meaning of the word "pampered," but she did not like the sound of it, so she denied that she was a "pampered Meritz." As Mabel drew up to the porch to let Lyle and Lisetta out, she reemphasized her point: "Here we are, Prince Lyle and Princess Lisetta. Please tell your mother that I will be in as soon as I put the horse and sleigh away."

Lisetta delivered the "royal" message to Minnie and added that Walter was not in school today. "Er muss auch arbeiten," responded Minnie, who was upstairs changing sheets on Lisetta's bed. Mabel's right, Minnie thought, as she looked at Lisetta's picture hanging above her bed. It had been taken two years before when Lisetta was three. She was dressed in a light blue dress of crepe de chine with a lace overlay. The skirt had accordion pleats all the way around, and the elbow-length puffy sleeves were tied with satin ribbons. Minnie had had the dress made for Lisetta by Ruth Fletcher, who was the best dressmaker in Hoskins.

The first time Lisetta wore the dress was on a Saturday in May, when the peonies were blooming in the garden. Gus and Minnie were taking Lyle and Lisetta to Norfolk to have their pictures taken by a photographer. Lyle was dressed in knee pants, a white shirt, a jacket, and a little red bow tie. Lisetta was in her fancy dress and her white high-top shoes. Minnie had curled her hair with a curling iron and had tied it back with a satin bow. For the finishing touch, she had gone out to the garden and had picked a huge pink peony for Lisetta to hold.

"Now, come look," she had said, leading Lisetta into her bedroom, where a full-length mirror hung on the back of the door. Lisetta stared at herself in the mirror; she touched the dress and felt her hair; she smelled the peony, which she held up to her dress. Looking in the mirror, she pranced around admiring herself. Minnie smiled, remembering Lisetta's vision of herself.

When it was almost time for supper, Mabel called the "little princess" to help prepare the supper, which would include smoked sausage, sauerkraut, and boiled potatoes.

"I can set the table," volunteered Lisetta. This was her job when Minnie prepared the meal.

"That's too easy," said Mabel. "You can peel these potatoes." She handed Lisetta a bowl of potatoes and a paring knife.

"I'll cut myself," said Lisetta.

"Not if you learn how." Mabel took the knife and skillfully pared the peelings off a large potato. "Here, you try now." Mabel handed her the knife. Lisetta worked slowly and carefully. She wanted to show Mabel that she could do it without cutting herself.

"I wish Walter could come to school more often," she said to Mabel.

"He gets to come more often than the rest of us did. He's the baby of the family."

"He doesn't act like a baby," Lisetta commented.

"Well, he hasn't always been the baby. Robert was the last one born. But he died when he was eighteen months old."

"Was he sick?"

"No. He had an accident. One morning when we were all busy talking and eating our breakfast, Robert crawled down from his chair without any of us noticing. He saw some biscuits sitting on top of the stove and crawled up to get one. On his way back down, his suspenders got caught on the spout of the teakettle, and he pulled the boiling water on top of himself."

"Oooh, how painful that must have been."

"Ja. Most of the water landed on his stomach and chest. He lived for two weeks, and before dying. "

"Couldn't Doctor Scheng help him?"

"No, all he could do was to give Robert some medicine to ease his pain."

"Poor Robert," said Lisetta.

"When Robert died, Father was very angry at God, and he hasn't been to church since. And Mother became very quiet. I think she blames herself for Robert's death."

"Poor Robert," repeated Lisetta.

"Yes, poor Robert and lucky Walter. Walt is the baby again now, and sometimes he gets spoiled, like you do."

After supper, Lisetta helped Mabel with the dishes. Then it was Lisetta's bedtime. Not long after Lisetta went upstairs, Mabel came up to tuck her in bed. As she turned down the kerosene lamp, she looked at the picture above Lisetta's bed.

"There's that little prissy princess. Good night, princess!" Lisetta's feelings were hurt. Mabel had been in a bad mood all day. She had called her a baby, a pampered Meritz, and a prissy princess. And Lisetta had tried so hard to please Mabel.

"I peeled all of those potatoes for you tonight," she said timidly.

"Yes, you did," admitted Mabel. "Well, goodnight, little potato peeler."

Lisetta smiled. Mabel had finally said something nice to her.

* * *

Most of the time, Lisetta tried very hard to please her superiors. She had tried to please Miss Martin all year at school. When summertime came, she had only Gus and Minnie to please, and Gus was always congenial. Minnie was more difficult. She was determined to prepare Lisetta for life as a farmer's wife, and she knew from personal experience that a good farmer's wife works harder than the farmer himself. Sometimes that meant that Lisetta had to stay home to work while Lyle went off to have fun with his father. This was the case on July 4th, 1918. Lyle was going with Gus to the carnival and patriotic celebration at Wayne. Lisetta pleaded to go along, and Gus did his best to persuade Minnie, but Minnie needed Lisetta to help her in the kitchen. Minnie always prepared a special meal for each holiday, and that meant that the butter had to be churned. A holiday meal demanded fresh butter.

"You know your job is to churn the butter, Zettie, so stop begging to go."

"No!"

"Go to your room, Zettie!"

Lisetta was full of anger for her mother. She went to the stairs and stomped hard on the first step with one foot and then stomped again with the other. Then she stepped up to the next step and stomped on it twice, and then each step in turn. Minnie let her get all of the way to the top and then said, "Now, Zettie, you come right back down here and go up those steps again like a lady." Lisetta obeyed, but she stayed in her room and sulked until Minnie called her down to churn the butter.

In preparation for the butter churning today, Minnie had saved up the cream from several days' milking. She poured the cream into the tall, cylindrical, ceramic butter churner, put the long wooden handle of the paddle through the wooden top, and placed the top on the churner. Lisetta sat on the kitchen steps to do the churning. From this height, she could pull the paddle up and down more easily. After an hour, the liquid began to separate into buttermilk and butter. When the paddle became almost impossible to pull up and down, she knew that the butter was firm. Minnie took the heavy container and poured off the buttermilk into a pail. She left Lisetta to wash the butter while she took the buttermilk out to the chickens.

Lisetta put the butter into a basin of cold water. Then she squeezed and washed and squeezed and washed, and poured off the water, poured on fresh water, and squeezed and washed again and again. She knew that she couldn't take any shortcuts with this part. Minnie had warned her time and again that if every bit of buttermilk was not removed, the butter would not stay sweet and fresh.

Finally, the butter was ready for salting. Lisetta added a handful of salt and kneaded the salt into the butter. Then she placed the large chunk of butter on a plate, molded it into a shape (this was her favorite part), and took it down into the fruit cellar. For this evening's meal and throughout the week, whenever butter was needed, she would be sent to the cellar to cut off a chunk of the butter.

When Lisetta finished with the butter, she peeled the potatoes for Minnie, strung the green beans, and set the table. Meanwhile, Minnie baked a peach pie and several loaves of bread and prepared the fryers.

Minnie had actually begun the preparation for fried chicken in the spring. Her goal was to have her first fryers for 4th of July dinner. Already in April, she had been watching her hens to see which ones were clucking a lot. This was a sign that they wanted to rear chicks. She prepared a nest of clean straw for each hen in separate wire cages. In early May, she placed the cluckers in their cages and allowed them to sit on their nests until their eggs were hatched. For a day or two after hatching, the young chicks ate the yolks from the broken egg shells. Then Minnie fed them with mash several times a day. Each day while the hens were out of their cages, watching over their chicks, Minnie changed the straw so that it would be fresh and clean, to avoid disease. At the end of the day, she shooed each hen and her chicks back into their cages for safekeeping during the night.

All of her hard work paid off in July when the first leghorns were ready to be butchered. The lucky pullets escaped death; they would be kept for laying eggs. But the unfortunate young roosters were at the mercy of Minnie's ax all summer long. On July 4th, she caught and butchered the first two pullets for dinner.

 At six o'clock, when Gus and Lyle returned from the celebration, everything was ready. Minnie served her holiday dinner with pride. Gus took a bite of fried chicken and then a bite of fresh bread and butter. "Alles schmeckt," he remarked, looking first at Minnie and then at Lisetta.

Shortly after the 4th of July, it was time to harvest the oats. This was a job for the entire neighborhood. Since none of the farmers owned their own binders or threshers, several weeks were set aside each summer when the itinerant operators of the binding and threshing machines came to service all of the farmers in the neighborhood.

To get this all done in a short period of time meant hard work for each farmer and his family. The binder came first and cut the oats, gathering the oats into shocks and tying them with binder twine. As the shocks were dropped onto the ground, the farmers walked behind the binder, picked up three shocks at a time and made a standing teepee out of them, with the oat kernels forming the top of the teepee and the stems forming the sides. In case it rained before the thresher came, the rain would drip down the sides of the teepees, and the tops would soon dry out, keeping the kernels from rotting. The teepee position was also the right position for the threshing machine to pick up the shocks.

After all of the binding had been done in the neighborhood, the thresher came around to complete the harvest. As the operator ran the machine, the farmers loaded the shocks onto hayracks and then pitched the shocks into the machine, which removed the kernels from the shocks and blew the kernels into wagons. Finally, the farmers drove the wagons of oat kernels to their storage bins and scooped in the oats.

When the binding and threshing took place at a neighbor's farm, Gus and Lyle helped out in the fields. But when these operations took place at their own farm, Minnie and Lisetta were needed as well. It was their responsibility to prepare the food for the entire crew.

The day before the harvest at the Meritzes, Mabel came to help. She and Minnie baked ten loaves of bread, four cakes, and six pies. Lisetta helped to prepare the fruit for the pies, working alongside Mabel. They worked in silence. Minnie believed that work is work and visiting is visiting, and mixing the two was "verboten."

On the day of the harvest, Minnie, Mabel and Lisetta began their work shortly after daylight. By eleven o'clock the field workers would be ravenous, and the meal needed to be ready. Minnie put into the oven large joints of pork, beef, and ham to roast. Mabel and Lisetta peeled dozens of potatoes, cut them up, and put them into salt water in a large bucket. Then they strung beans, shelled peas, scraped carrots, and cut up fresh tomatoes from the garden. Minnie made huge pots of coffee and chopped ice from a big block to cool large pitchers of water.

Since there would be too many workers to eat indoors, Minnie and Mabel set up long boards on trestles on the lawn and took chairs and benches outside. They covered the makeshift table with tablecloths and set it with plates, cups, glasses, utensils, and napkins.

Shortly before eleven o'clock, Minnie mashed the potatoes and made gravy. It was Mabel's job to carry out the heavy bowls and serving plates of food and Lisetta's job to bring the empty ones in for replenishing.

Finally, when the men started on their dessert, Minnie came outside. She didn't want to miss the compliments she knew she would get on her food. Gus did not compliment her today. He left it to their neighbors: "Wonderful food," said Mr. Spangler. "The best we've had all week," added Mr. Muller.

"Danke," answered Minnie. "Have some more!" Mr. Muller shook his head, touched his stomach, and rolled his eyes in pretended agony. His neighbors laughed at his antics. In spite of the hard work during the harvest, they were enjoying each other's company.

When they went back to the fields, Minnie, Mabel, and Lisetta ate their dinner and then washed and dried all of the dishes. It seemed to Lisetta that the stack of dishes never got any smaller. But finally, Mabel handed her the last plate to dry.

"May I go play now, Ma?"

"No, Zettie, we have to fix the lunch for the workers."

Lisetta knew what that meant: countless sandwiches of left-over roast pork, beef, and ham, and fresh strawberries, cake, and gallons of lemonade. While Minnie fixed all of the sandwiches and wrapped them in damp dish towels, Mabel and Lisetta removed the stems from the strawberries and squeezed lemons until their wrists ached.

"Now may I go play, Ma?"

"Halt dein Mund, Zettie! We have to get this lunch out to the field by four o'clock."

Minnie got her clothes basket and placed the sandwiches in it. "Just a minute," she said as she wiped her hands on her apron. She took a dish towel that was still damp from all of the noon dishes, folded it into a band, wrapped it around her forehead and the back of her head, and tied it very tightly.

"You look like an Indian, Ma."

"Well, I feel like I've got a woodpecker inside my head."

Minnie hitched up the cart to Beauty. She and Mabel loaded the clothes basket, the heavy containers of lemonade, the bucket of strawberries, and the cakes onto the cart. Lisetta hopped on, and they all headed for the field.

The crew in the fields saw them coming and were glad to stop their work in the hot July sun. Gus took off his straw hat, mopped his brow with his handkerchief, put his hat back on, plopped down on the ground, and motioned for Lisetta to join him.

"So, when are you going to sell those fat cattle of yours?" Mr. Spangler asked Gus.

"I don't know. The market is too low right now."'

"Gus is going to have a big problem if he doesn't sell those cattle soon," warned

Minnie "They're so fat, they just stay on the ground and moan."

Gus nodded his head in agreement. He had a dilemma on his hands. He couldn't keep the cattle much longer, and he couldn't afford to sell them. However, he knew exactly what the market needed to be for him to make a profit. Although he could not read, he had taught himself to calculate. He had become a whiz at arithmetic, and he had trained himself to keep good records of the amount and cost of the feed and of the original cost of the animals. He had also become an excellent judge of weight. From looking at a steer, he could tell within a pound the weight of the large creature.   So; he had all of the information he needed to make a decision regarding profit and loss. He had only to wait until the market was up.

A week later, Gus called the auction house at Omaha to check on cattle prices. Minnie was cooking at the stove. "Gut! The market is up!" yelled Gus. "If the truckers can pick the cattle up yet today, we can sell them tomorrow. Want to go to Omaha, Minnie?" Minnie thought a minute; the oats harvest was over; she had worked hard; she could get Hank to do the milking the next morning. "Ja!" she answered joyfully.

It would be one hundred and twenty miles from Hoskins to Omaha. Although they would pass through many small towns – Wisner, West Point, Hooper – and Fremont, a larger town, they wouldn't stop to eat.

In the morning Minnie fixed up a basket with bread, ham, and Kaffeekuchen and filled a container with coffee. Lisetta and Lyle fell asleep in the backseat almost immediately. It was still dark, and the air was heavy with summer humidity, adding to the stupor of their young, sleepy bodies. Minnie was excited. It had been a while since she had made this trip with Gus, and Gus was driving sensibly today. She handed him pieces of food or cups of coffee as they drove towards Omaha.

At five o'clock, the horizon began to glow. Minnie could see the dark outline of the hills in front of the crescent of the reddish-yellow rising sun. In a few minutes the whole sun was visible, and the dark hills had turned to emerald green. Now Minnie could see the landscape to the right and the left as they traveled. She examined the countryside with a critical eye: a field of corn that had been planted too late; a pasture that needed mowing; a barn needing repair; a meadow full of musk thistles. Suddenly, a lovely farmhouse caught her attention.

"Look at that, Gus! It's like ours!"

"Not as nice," Gus answered. "It doesn't have you to look after it. By the way, Minnie, while Lyle and I are at the auction today, I want you and Zettie to go shopping for a piano. I'll be buying calves if I see some good, healthy-looking ones, but there should be plenty of money left over from the sale of the steers."

As they approached Omaha, most of the vehicles on the road were automobiles and trucks. There were four lanes of traffic, with stop signs at almost every intersection. Lisetta looked up at the tall buildings, some seven or eight stories high. Gus dropped Minnie and Lisetta at a hotel where they could freshen up and wait until the stores opened. Then he and Lyle headed for the auction barn. They turned off from Dodge Street and drove towards the river.

"That river is awfully wide!" exclaimed Lyle as he caught sight of it.

"Ja," answered Gus. "It's called the wi**de** Missouri. It flows along here between Omaha and Council Bluffs on the other side – and then it flows into the Mississippi River, which is even wider, I understand."

Not far from the river were the stockyards. As they approached, they could hear the constant noise of complaining cattle. Gus did not think of the happiness of his cattle today. He was interested in how much he could sell them for and how little he would have to pay for his next herd. Also, he wanted to give Lyle a lesson in judging the weight, age, and health of cattle. Before they went into the auction house, they walked through a part of the stockyard and discussed the animals.

Meanwhile, Minnie and Lisetta were busy shopping. Their first stop was a clothing store, where Minnie purchased items for Lyle and Lisetta for school in the fall. The next stop was a jewelry store, where she purchased a new watch chain for Gus and a pin for herself. Their final stop was the Steinway piano store. Minnie had heard that Steinways were the best. Lisetta was amazed at the size of the grand pianos, but Minnie remained calm as a salesman explained the differences between a baby grand, a parlor grand, and a concert grand. He demonstrated the sound of each. Minnie knew what she wanted – the black parlor grand would look impressive in her living room. Minnie wrote the price on the back of the salesman's card, thanked him, and headed back to the hotel.

When she and Lisetta entered the lobby, Gus and Lyle were already waiting. By Gus's expression, Minnie could tell that he had not done as well as he had expected.

"I got a good price on the calves I bought," he said, "but the market was down from yesterday. We made money on the cattle, but only a small profit."

"Well," answered Minnie, "that should teach you not to hold out for such a fat price. Think of all the money you could have saved on feed."

Gus grimaced. "How did you do, Minnie?"

"Some clothes and jewelry, but the Steinway I liked is expensive." She handed him the salesman's card.

"Hm, we can't afford that now – perhaps in a few years."

* * *

A week later, the Gus Meritz family were again working together – this time in the alfalfa pasture. The prairie meadow had been mowed for the season, and the alfalfa had already been mowed once, but it had grown enough by now to be mowed a second time. They started out

26

early in the morning. Minnie hitched up to a wagon a team of horses that included Nellie, who was the oldest and gentlest of the horses. Lisetta's job was to ride Nellie and to call, "Giddup!" and "Whoa!" Minnie drove another horse, which pulled a scythe. As she cut the alfalfa with the scythe, Gus raked the hay into rows; Lyle pitched the alfalfa onto the wagon; Hank, who usually helped on these occasions, stood on top of the wagon and stacked the hay as Lyle pitched it up. When the wagon was full, Lisetta drove the team to the barn or to a location for a haystack, and Hank dumped the stack.

Lisetta enjoyed alfalfa cutting in comparison to oats harvesting. Instead of the endless hours of peeling potatoes, washing vegetables, and doing dishes, she was out in the sunshine, riding obedient Nellie and sniffing the sweet perfume of the alfalfa.

"So, Zettie," Gus said at the end of the day, "how would you like to do that all over in about six weeks when the alfalfa needs cutting again?"

"I'd like to," answered Lisetta, "but what about the prairie meadow? Won't it need to be cut again?"

"Well, there're different kinds of grass. Alfalfa is fast growing; so, we can cut it for hay more than once in a season. You can get a lot of hay from an alfalfa pasture. Also, it's good for the soil. You can sow alfalfa seeds in a field to give the soil a rest from corn or oats. After a few years, the alfalfa can be plowed under and the grain planted again in good, rich soil."

"I see. You don't ever plant corn or oats in a prairie meadow?"

"No. There aren't very many prairie meadows left in this area. The ones that have been left are ones where the land isn't good enough to grow grain. So, they're just left untouched. But as long as machinery doesn't come in and rip them up, the prairie grass comes back faithfully every spring, and it's always sweet and good for the cattle to eat."

"That's nice," said Lisetta. "I hope no one ever plows up our prairie meadow."

"No one will as long as I'm here," promised Gus.

Chapter 4: Lessons

In the fall of 1918, Lisetta was in the second grade at District 60, and Walter was in the eighth. The eighth graders were studying the geography and history of Nebraska. Walter, who already had a love of the land, enjoyed first reading about Nebraska in his textbook and then listening to Miss Martin as she explained and discussed the text.

Miss Martin began this unit of study with information about the Homestead Act, which was passed by Congress in 1862: Any citizen or alien who declared the intention of becoming a citizen, if he was twenty-one years old or the head of a family, could pay ten dollars and file a claim for not more than one hundred and sixty acres of surveyed public domain. If he "resided upon or cultivated" the land for five years, became a citizen, and paid additional fees, the homestead became his and could not be seized by a creditor to satisfy any previously contracted debts.

Since there was no legal provision in the Homestead Act for free transportation to the land, prospective farmers had to pay their own way. Not many farmers could acquire the necessary capital for that or for an investment in housing, implements, fences, and livestock. If they could get to the land, they were at the mercy of the weather, their harsh environment, and their isolation. Consequently, only one in three homesteaders managed to remain long enough to get deeds to their farms. By 1900, the bulk of the fertile land with abundant rainfall had been purchased by big land speculators, who rented it out to tenant farmers or resold the land to latecomers at $1.25 per acre.

* * *

The next unit of study was about the early inhabitants of Nebraska: The earliest inhabitants of the area were the five tribes of Plains Indians: The Sioux, who were warriors, were the most feared horsemen of the Plains. The Kiowas were buffalo hunters and also owned large herds of horses. The Pawnee were earth lodgers and farmers, but also hunters and raiders. Like the Pawnee, the Omaha were earth lodgers in the spring and autumn. During the hunting seasons, they moved into teepees and ranged about. The Otoes were dwellers along the Missouri and the Platte rivers. The name "Nebraska" is derived from the Oto Indian word meaning "flat water," which was their description of the Platte River.

The earliest white people in the area were the fur trappers, who were sometimes called "Mountain Men." From 1824, they followed the Platte River to their trapping grounds in the mountain regions west of Nebraska. John Jacob Neihardt, Nebraska's famous poet, wrote a long narrative poem called "The Song of Hugh Glass," which describes how a mountain man is attacked by a grisly bear, who mauls him so badly that the man must try to crawl back to his home base. Miss Martin explained to the eighth-graders that they could look forward to reading the poem when they got to high school. She with the history of the pioneers.

Beginning in 1841, thousands of emigrants began passing through Nebraska. They followed the south bank of the Platte River, known as the Oregon Trail, en route to Colorado, Utah, California, and Oregon. Congress established the Nebraska Territory in 1854. Most of the early pioneer settlements were along the Missouri River. Bellevue, the oldest, was followed by Omaha. Then settlements began to spring up west of the Missouri, at Plattsmouth, West Point, Beatrice, Columbus, Falls City, and Fremont.

While the settlers were moving into the area, the Omaha Indians were being moved onto a reservation. (Miss Martin rolled down a map of Nebraska, hanging above the blackboard, and pointed out the location of the reservation: an area fifty miles north of Omaha, bordered by the Missouri River on the east.) Eleven years later, the Winnebago Indians from the Wisconsin/Illinois area were forced to move onto a reservation bordering the Omaha reservation on the north.

With the construction of the Union Pacific railway in 1865-1869, railroad and cow towns grew up at Grand Island, Hastings, and Kearney. In 1867, Congress passed the Nebraska Statehood Bill, proclaiming Nebraska the thirty-seventh state of the union. The first Nebraska state legislature located their capital at the little village of Lancaster, which they later renamed Lincoln.

At the time that Nebraska became a state, almost all of the settlements were still located in the southeastern portion of the state, south of the Platte River. The exceptions were West Point, Wisner, Columbus, and North Fork. North Fork, which had just been settled the previous year, in 1866, was eventually renamed Norfolk. (Miss Martin's pronunciation of Norfolk – "Naw-fork" – was the typical local pronunciation, which sounded like a combination of the two.

*   *   *

"Did you know that Omaha is a lot older than Norfolk?" Walter asked that evening at suppertime.

"You mean as a city?" responded Mabel.

"Ja. North Fork, as it used to be called, wasn't even here until 1866."

"Huh," said Mabel. "So that's what you're learning in eighth grade."

The following day, Miss Martin told her students how North Fork had been chosen as a spot for settlement: In a sense, Fredrick William III, the King of Prussia, was responsible for the settlement of North Fork. He was adamant that no religious differences should separate the people of his country. When he forced the Lutheran and the Reformed churches into a single body, many of his subjects rebelled. In 1843, after a stormy seven-week voyage, a group of one hundred and fifty Prussian Lutherans arrived at New York from Hamburg. From there, they headed west to Buffalo, Milwaukee, and Ixonia in the Territory of Wisconsin. The group settled down and established themselves with property, a church, and a school.

By 1865, so many new immigrants had come to Ixonia, there was little good land to be had around the church. The young people were forced to leave the area to seek new territory. Some of them moved to Minnesota. However, shocking reports came back about warring Indians. Fort Ridgely had been burned; women and children at Essig had been dismembered; forty-two Indians had been hanged on a scaffold. Although the Indian uprisings were temporarily put down, no one wanted to go to Minnesota to settle.

Pastor Hoeckendorf, the head of St. Paul's Lutheran Church in Ixonia, had relatives near West Point, in the Nebraska area. They wrote him that there was still good land to be had in the area – prairie land which could be farmed without first needing to cut down timber and pull up stumps.

In the summer of 1865, the congregation from Ixonia sent Frederick Wagner, Herman Braasch, and John Gensmer to scout the area around West Point. They went from Chicago to St. Joseph, Missouri by train and from there to Omaha on a Missouri River ferry boat. From there they travelled on foot. On September 15, 1865, the three scouts camped at the spot where the Elkhorn River is met by its north fork. This spot had everything they were looking for: good land, wood, excellent drinking water, and plenty of grass. When they returned to Ixonia in late fall, they gave a glowing report of the spot to their family and friends. During the winter, a group of congregants made preparations for the journey the following spring.

When Miss Martin continued the lesson the next day, she described the journey from Ixonia to North Fork: On May 23, 1866, forty-two covered wagons and one hundred and twenty-five people, divided into three groups, began their long journey. They had to carry with them everything they would need: food, clothing, utensils, tools, grain, and animals. Each family had a wagon drawn by four oxen. The men drove the oxen; the women and the children walked alongside, herding the cows and the sheep; babies were carried like papooses.

The wagon trains moved slowly, crossing southern Wisconsin and the entire length of Iowa, almost six hundred miles before they reached the Nebraska Territory. Once a week they halted to allow the men to hunt while the women washed, ironed, and baked bread. The wild game which the men brought in from their hunts was a welcome change from their usual food – bread and milk soup. To make the soup, they milked the cows directly into their big iron kettles, put the kettles over their campfires, and "rivelled" flour into the boiling milk. On Sundays, they rested and worshipped.

August Braasch, one of the leaders of the journey, kept a notebook of places enroute, along with occasional comments about their trip. (Miss Martin read out a few items from a copy of the notebook.)

Ixonia

Jefferson

Monroe – very hilly

Mississippi River

Catfish – 2 mile house

White Water – hilly

Cedar Rapids – sandy

Des Moines City

Baked on Sunday – forgive us, Lord!

Braasch's horse died.

Missouri River

Omaha, Nebraska

When the land was hilly or sandy, the wagons had to be unloaded and the provisions carried by the men to a spot where the oxen could again handle the load. When they came to the Mississippi and later to the Missouri, they again had to unload their provisions onto rafts in order to get across.

Finally, on July 12, 1866, their fifty-day journey came to an end on the banks of the Elkhorn River. The entire company joined in prayer, thanking God for having brought them safely to their new home.

*   *   *

When Walter went home from school, he described this journey at the supper table.

> "Just think," he said, "Lyle and Lisetta's grandparents, the Bechs, were among these early pioneers!"

> "So that's why they're so proud!" retorted Mabel.

Walter, who also had a love of building, found the unit the next day even more fascinating: The pioneers agreed upon a division of the land along the Elkhorn River. They arranged themselves on either side of the river, on quarter sections four times as long as they were wide, with the width portion adjacent to the river. In this way each man's stock could have easy access to water, and the whole colony could easily band together in case of an attack by the Indians. The local Pawnees were peaceful, but marauding Sioux roamed the area.

31

The families continued to live in their covered wagons while they helped each other to build dwellings. Some built dugouts in hillsides, shoring up the earth inside with the wood from their torn-apart wagons. Some cut blocks of sod and laid them in horizontal layers to form sod houses. Some cut down timber along the river banks and constructed one-room log huts. They made the roofs for the sod houses and the log huts out of willow thongs and reeds, which grew abundantly in the lowland by the river. They lashed the reeds and the willow thongs together and then covered them with sod. The dugouts were windowless, but some of the sod houses and the log huts had single half-windows, which were a luxury item. Glass for the windows required a trip to Omaha, as did other building materials, such as nails.

Until the settlers could stockpile grain and produce, they had to travel long distances for food supplies: thirty-five miles to Wisner, fifty miles to Columbus. Getting flour meant a three-day trip to West Point. Hauling grain was a tedious task. Because roads were so poor, wagons had to be unloaded and reloaded many times during a single trip.

Although it was already late in the planting season when the settlers arrived, they tried to plant potatoes and beans. But they found that their cast-iron stump plows were useless in the prairie land. They had to dig and plant by hand and were able to get in only a small crop, not enough to see them through the winter.

The winter of 1867 was a harsh one. Many of the fathers and older sisters left their families and went to Fremont or Omaha for jobs. They traveled home again in early spring with much-needed supplies.

Miss Martin laid her notes down on her desk. "To be continued," she said to her class. The students groaned in protest and begged her to go on. Miss Martin smiled, shook her head, and pointed to the wall clock. "Four o-clock. Time to go."

Walter had to wait until Monday to hear the rest of the story: The spring of 1867 was beautiful – plenty of rain and sunshine. The weather remained good throughout the summer, and by fall the settlers had an abundant supply of food and grain. In thanksgiving to God, they built the first church in the North Fork area, St. Paul's Lutheran Church. It was a joint effort. Some of the men traveled eighty miles to Fremont to purchase pine logs which they sawed into lumber at West Point on their way home. Fifty men drove teams of four oxen to the area which is now Battle Creek, where they cut down huge cottonwoods and then dragged them back to the site of the future church. Other men cut down willow trees along the river banks.

The church they built was twenty by thirty feet. They used cottonwood logs for the corner posts and the beams of the church and the pine lumber for the walls. They fashioned the roof out of green willow branches and reeds covered with sod. For the floor they laid down branches of willow trees and covered them with straw.

This building also doubled as the first school in the area. Pastor Hoeckendorf was both the preacher and the teacher, preaching on Sunday and teaching during the week, both in the

German language. In addition to the church, the first sorghum mill was built in 1867 by the Hille family. Now the settlers could have their sweet Kaffeekuchen, which they had missed since sugar could not easily be acquired. In 1868 the first post office was built, and the settlers no longer had to travel to West Point for their mail. Now it was easier to communicate with friends and relatives in Wisconsin and elsewhere.

Each spring wagon trains of new settlers arrived. As the community grew, it radiated out from North Fork: northeast to Hoskins, Winside and Wayne, southeast to Stanton, south to Madison, west to Battle Creek, northwest to Hadar and Pierce.

The Hoskins area was primarily settled by friends and relatives of those first settlers at North Fork, and the ties between the two communities have remained close. In 1886 Trinity Evangelical Lutheran Church in Hoskins was started by its "mother" church, St. Paul's, in North Fork. Ten years later, the Hoskins congregation had grown large enough to support its own pastor.

"Any questions?" asked Miss Martin.

Walter raised his hand and asked, "Why was North Fork changed to Norfolk?"

"That was a mistake. When the city was being incorporated, the name North Fork was put on the charter papers, but someone in Washington, D.C. misread the papers and registered the name as Norfolk. When the charter came back with the wrong name, the local people didn't want to go through the whole procedure again. So North Fork became Norfolk."

*   *   *

Miss Martin was superior to the average country school teacher, partly because of her youth and enthusiasm and partly because her fiancé was serving as a soldier in Europe. She used The Norfolk Daily News and letters from her fiancé to broaden her students' knowledge of the war in Europe. She wanted them to be prepared if any of their family members were called up to serve.

Miss Martin began with the sinking of the Lusitania: When the Lusitania was sunk by a German submarine in 1915, some Americans were ready to enter the war at that time. The Hoskins German farmers were not. They were torn between the attack on their new country and the concern they had for relatives in Germany. But when they could no longer send letters back and forth to relatives, they knew that they had become full-fledged Americans.

The United States entered the war in April of 1917. The first of the Hoskins boys to die on the battlefield was Ernest Bech. His body was shipped back home to be buried in the Lutheran Cemetery, not far from the Bech mausoleum.

By the time the United States entered the war, the Allied forces had grown to almost four million men against two and a half million Germans. However, the German land defense, under the leadership of Ludendorff, was more successful than the Allied forces. Ludendorff thinned out his front defense against the Allied forces and used his men for prompt local counter attacks and for manning the concrete pillboxes, which were armed with deadly machine guns.

Miss Martin used the war names to teach lessons in geography. She placed markers on the map of Europe at the locations where battles had taken place. For a while, the markers moved west as Ludendorff took the offense and marched his troops towards the Atlantic Ocean. At first, the war names were Arras and Saint Quentin, La Fere, Somme, Vimy, Avre, Hazebrouck, Marne, Chateau-Thierry, and finally Flanders.

After Flanders, Ludendorff made the mistake of allowing his troops a period of rest and preparation before delivering what he thought would be the final blow to the British. But he underestimated the power and the will of the British forces and the strength of the Allied tank divisions. The Allies pushed back the Germans in Flanders and regained the offensive. Now the markers moved east on the map as the Allied forces began attacking the Germans on all fronts: Reims, Briery, Metz, the Balkans, Salonika, Megiddo, Damascus, Aleppo.

On October third, 1918, the German government appealed for an immediate armistice. While the government was debating the conditions of the armistice, the fighting continued. The Allied forces simultaneously pushed on several fronts. There were attacks by the Americans west of the Meuse, by the French west of the Argonne, by the British in the direction of Mauberge, and by the Belgians in the direction of Ghent.

But Ludendorff managed to retreat faster than the Allies could pursue. Once again, he became optimistic. He wanted a temporary armistice now, one just long enough to give his troops a rest. This was discouraging news to the Hoskins community. More of their young men would be called up before this slaughter was over.

*   *   *

In early October, Lisetta came home from school with news. She was in a mood of tense excitement. "Walter told us at school today that Hank has been called up for the army."

"Oh, no!" exclaimed Minnie.

"Ja, he has to leave in early November for Chicago. They're sending him to training camp."

Gus knew that it would not be long before Mr. Getzmer came over to deliver the news personally. And, sure enough, as the Meritzes were finishing their supper, Wilhelm knocked on the door. Gus invited him into the dining room.

"I got apple pie," said Minnie. "Can I get you a piece?"

Wilhelm had already had bread pudding at home, but he couldn't pass up a piece of Minnie's pie. As he ate, he complained about the war. "Dieser verdammte Ludendorff! He's killing all zeh young Germans, und now he vants to kill all zeh young Americans. Vee came to America to get avay from zeh fighting, und now my boy has to go to fight."

"Perhaps all of the fighting will be over by the time Hank gets there. They keep talking about an armistice."

"I don't trust zatt Ludendorff. Er ist verruckt in dem Kopf."

"Can you get letters through to your family?" asked Gus.

"Nein." Wilhelm got up from the table and began pacing about the dining room, gesturing with his hands as he expressed his anger about the war and his fear for his brother Richard and his mother. For all he knew, they were starving or had been driven out of their home or they were dead.

"You must pray for them, Herr Getzmer," said Gus.

"Humph! I gave that up a long time ago."

"Well, I'll pray for them," Gus retorted.

"I really came to talk about Hank," said Wilhelm. He explained that Hank would want to work on Minnie's farm again if he returned. In the meantime, his other boys could do Hank's work.

"It's Minnie's farm," said Gus. "What do you think, Minnie?"

"That's fine with me. I get along well with Paul and Emil. Just don't send me Dick or Ferd."

"Now, Minnie," chided Gus. "They're all Herr Getzmer's boys."

"Ach, es macht nichts," said Wilhelm, smiling. "I know my boys."

"When does Hank leave?" asked Minnie.

"November der Zehnte, from zeh Hoskins depot."

"We'll be there to say good-bye."

*   *   *

Still the Germans pushed on. Austria collapsed. On November third, the Austrians signed an armistice. The Allies were demanding an unconditional surrender from the Germans, but Ludendorff attempted to carry on the struggle in hopes of a conditional surrender. On November fourth, revolution broke out in Germany. The people called for the Kaiser to abdicate and for Ludendorff to resign. Finally on November ninth, Prince Max resigned to the socialist, Friedrich Ebert, and Germany became a republic.

On the morning of November tenth, Germany had not yet signed an armistice. The Meritzes headed for Hoskins to see Hank off at the depot. When they got there, the depot was crowded with the Getzmer's neighbors, many of the town folk, and the entire Getzmer family. Hank was embarrassed to be the center of so much attention. He shuffled back and forth, listening to good wishes and advice from friends and relatives. When he saw the train finally approaching from the direction of Norfolk, he was relieved. The train stopped just long enough to unload goods and to pick up passengers. Hank hugged his father and his brothers and kissed his sisters and his mother. As he stepped onto the train, Minnie handed him a basket full of her freshly baked Kaffeekuchen.

"Take good care of your mother, Zettie," Hank yelled as the train pulled out.

The train to Chicago stopped at every small town along the way. The first three stops were familiar ones to Hank: Winside, where he had grown up; Wayne, the county seat, where he sometimes went on farm business; and Sioux City, where he had been to the cattle auction. After that, all of the little Iowa towns meant nothing to him. They all looked the same – a collection of small frame houses scattered randomly on either side of the tracks, a small depot with an open-sided platform sheltered by a roof suspended on pillars, and a small café next to the depot. After several hours, Hank took advantage of one of the stops to get a cup of coffee to go with Minnie's coffee cake.

Back in the train, the constant clickety-click of the train wheels made Hank sleepy. He propped his head up against the window with a pillow and fell asleep. As the train wound its way through Iowa and into Illinois, history was changing with each mile. When the train crossed the border, it came to a stop, and Hank awoke. It was seven o'clock in the morning, later than he usually slept. He was hungry and thirsty, so he went into the café to get a sandwich and a cup of coffee. As Hank stood in line, waiting his turn, a man suddenly burst into the café, waving a telegram.

"The war is over!" he yelled. "Germany signed the armistice!"

The passengers broke out in cheers. Strangers hugged each other. The station master rang a bell. When the merriment had subsided a little, Hank sat down with his sandwich and coffee and wondered whether to go back home or to continue on to Chicago and report to the military. He decided that he had better report. In Chicago he was met by an army sergeant, who told him to turn around and go back home. But after his big sendoff, Hank was embarrassed to return home so soon. He decided to postpone the return by paying a visit to his Uncle Herman, who had recently moved his family to Chicago from Cleveland.

A week later, when Hank's train pulled into the Hoskins depot, he stepped off and immediately headed for the country road that led to home. Fortunately, he met no friends on the three-mile trek to the farm. As he stood at the top of the hill and looked down the lane leading to his parents' home, he saw none of his family. His father and brothers were in the fields, and even the dog was not there to greet him.

Hank walked down the lane and set his suitcase on the porch. He opened the screen door quietly, wanting to surprise his mother, who was peeling potatoes at the kitchen sink.

"Ma, I'm home! The war is over!"

Emelia jumped and screamed. She ran to Hank, pulled his six-foot frame down to her petite five-foot level and kissed him, holding his cheeks in her hand.

"Mein lieber Knabe," she said. "Danke Gott!"

Chapter 5: Changes

Hank continued to work on Minnie's farm throughout the winter, but when spring came, he developed spring fever. He had had a taste of life outside the Hoskins community, and when his Uncle Herman wrote him and encouraged him to come to Chicago, Hank decided to go.

"I'll never see you again," Lisetta said tearfully when he broke the news to the Meritzes.

"Yes, you will! When you're all grown up, I'll see a lot of you. You just wait."

*   *   *

On her first day back to school in late August as a fifth grader, Lisetta walked alone through the alfalfa pasture. Lyle was now attending parochial school in Hoskins. She was happy; she would soon see her friends, Rose, Elsie and Walter, and her teacher, Miss Martin. As she walked along, she picked some of the cheerful yellow cowslips and some fragrant white Easter lilies, as she called them, because they first started blooming about Easter time.

When Lisetta entered the classroom, she held the bouquet behind her back to surprise Miss Martin. But Lisetta was the one surprised. Instead of Miss Martin, an older lady was seated at the teacher's desk. Miss Martin had left Hoskins!

"I'm Lisetta Meritz," she introduced herself, "and these are for you."

"Thank you. I'm Mrs. Bosen, and I'm allergic to prairie flowers. Please take them outside."

Lisetta was downcast. She thought: H*ow could anyone be allergic to prairie flowers? They're so pretty and smell so sweet.* She took the bouquet outside and laid it down on the steps. She planned to give it to Rose at recess time.

Mrs. Bosen was just the beginning of troubles for Lisetta that year.   First, there was the trouble with the bull, which Lisetta was afraid of. She had to walk through "his" pasture each day to and from school. He was no problem if he and his cows were off grazing on the hillside, but if they were at the bottom of the hill, close to where Lisetta walked, he became protective and snorted at her. She stayed close to the fence in case he charged. Lisetta finally shared her fear with Minnie, who took the trouble to Gus.

"Gus, I want you to get rid of that bull. He's mean!"

"He's not mean, Minnie. He's a bull."

"Well, he snorts at Zettie when she walks through the pasture, and he snorts at me, too, when I have to bring in the cows for milking. He follows along, and when the cows are being milked in the barn, he bangs his head against the side of the barn."

"He's harmless. He only has little stumps for horns. He has yet to charge at me when I wave my cap at him."

"You're an idiot, Gus."

Gus knew that Minnie could take care of herself, but he was concerned for Lisetta. On the other hand, since he did not want to sell the bull, he put him into the feedlot with the steers. Deprived of his cows and his freedom, the bull became even meaner

* * *

On a Saturday in October, Gus drove Minnie and Lisetta into Hoskins to catch the train for Norfolk. When he returned home, he checked to see what Lyle was doing and found him working in the blacksmith shop, pounding out a crooked plow blade.

"I'm going to feed the livestock," Gus informed Lyle.

Gus mixed the slop for the hogs, poured it into their troughs, and opened the door of the hog barn to let them in. Next, he pitched hay from the barn loft down into the stalls for the horses and cows. Then he headed for the feedlot. It had rained heavily during the night, and he wanted to make sure that the steers had salt. If they didn't lick the salt, they wouldn't drink water and gain weight as fast.

When Gus entered the feedlot, the bull was moping in a corner. He did not move as Gus waded through the mud to look at the salt trays. Gus determined that the salt trays were still full enough and began heading for the fence. The bull suddenly snorted and charged. Gus ran as fast as he could in his overshoes in the thick mud. When he reached the wooden fence, he tried to climb over, but he could not get his overshoes through the slats. Pinning Gus against the fence with his stubby horns, the bull had him trapped.

"Help!" Gus yelled at the top of his voice, beating the bull with his fists. "Help! Lyle!"

Lyle heard his father's cry and came running with his hammer. He beat the bull on the head again and again until he finally backed off. Shaken and badly bruised in the chest area, Gus walked through the gate and out of the feedlot.

"See," Minnie said that evening, "I told you that bull was mean."

"You were right, Minnie. I've called a trucker to take him to the cattle auction."

A few weeks later, Gus came home from the cattle auction with trouble he knew Minnie would not want to hear.

"Your brother Paul was the talk of the cattle barn today, Minnie."

Minnie expected to hear good news. Paul was an excellent judge of cattle, and many of the farmers regularly engaged him to buy and sell for them.

"It's not good news, Minnie. Paul sold a big herd of cattle for a farmer and ran off with the money."

"No! Where?"

"That's just it. No one knows. He left Bess and their two boys. Didn't even say goodbye."

"How awful! How could he do that?

"I guess there's a bad apple on the Bech tree."

"To tell the truth, I've always suspected that Paul was no good, and now he's a disgrace to our whole family." She paused. "But the Meritzes aren't perfect either, you know.

*   *   *

A month later, Gus proved just how imperfect he was. He had gone into Norfolk to shop for a new plow and had taken Lyle and Lisetta along to visit with Loretta and Engie at Ed and Ella's. When he finished shopping, he stopped in at the tavern on Third and Main for a few beers and a game of poker. It was already five-thirty when he picked up Lyle and Lisetta. Gus sped along quickly on the way home, knowing that Minnie would be upset if they were late for supper. There was almost no traffic on the road from Norfolk to Hoskins. When they got to Hoskins, Gus sped through the town and swung wide around the bend of the narrow country road. Unfortunately, Mr. Lieb was also driving as though he owned the road, and the two collided. Gus's Buick was thrown off the road, Lyle was jolted from the back seat into the front, and Lisetta hit her head on the door handle. As the door swung open, she fell out and rolled into the ditch.

"Dad, Zettie fell out," shouted Lyle.

"Ach, mein Gott!" exclaimed Gus.

They found Lisetta in the ditch with a surprised look on her face, shaken but unhurt. Banged up as it was, the car was still drivable, but they got home late for supper. Minnie demanded an explanation, and the truth came out.

"Gus, I've been telling you that you drive too fast."

"Ja, Minnie."

"And you smell like you've been in a beerhall."

"Ja, Minnie."

"And stop saying *Ja, Minnie.*"

"Ja, Minnie"

*   *   *

The next trouble came in the spring, several weeks before summer vacation – this time to both Lyle and Lisetta. Lyle came home from parochial school with a fever, a runny nose, and watery eyes. Inside his mouth were tiny white spots, like grains of salt. A day later, tiny red spots appeared, first on his forehead and behind his ears, then on the rest of his body until he was a mass of red. Lisetta's measles took the same course but started a week after Lyle's. Minnie pulled down the shades to darken their bedrooms and kept them in bed for several weeks.

"I'm missing all of the fifth-grade examinations, Ma," Lisetta complained. "I won't be promoted next year."

"Such foolishness!" responded Minnie. "All of your report cards have been very good. Now, stop worrying and go to sleep"

Chapter 6: Humility, Patience, and Courage

When Lisetta went back to school in the fall, she found that she had not been promoted to the sixth grade. She knew why; she had missed the examinations when she had the measles. Mrs. Bosen seated the students by class, and when Lisetta was placed with the fifth graders, she was mortified. She kept her head down, not allowing herself to look at any of the other students. The morning dragged on for her – nine-fifteen, nine-thirty, ten o'clock. Finally, at ten-fifteen, recess began, and she could talk to Mrs. Bosen.

"I know why I wasn't promoted," Lisetta said, "but all of my report cards were good. I know the fifth-grade material."

"But you didn't take the examination, Lisetta. Rules are rules."

"I was sick, Mrs. Bosen. I had the measles. But I can take the examination now."

"No. That wouldn't be fair to the other students. They didn't have all summer to study."

"I didn't study this summer. I worked on the farm."

"Stop arguing, Lisetta. You will stay in the fifth grade this year."

When Lisetta got home and told Minnie and Gus about this, Minnie was angry.

"She's a ridiculous woman. Who does she think she is, the Queen of Sheba?"

Gus was no help. "I never did like school," was all he said.

"Ma, I don't think I can go through a whole year as a fifth grader again. It's so embarrassing."

"You may have to, Zettie. I don't know what you can do about it right now."

Day after day Lisetta went to school with a heavy heart. School was no fun anymore. Rose and Elsie were still her friends, but now there were two grades between them. Lisetta felt foolish solving the same thought problems in arithmetic, reading the same stories, practicing the same spelling words.

"I'm not learning anything," she complained to Minnie.

"Yes, you are. You're learning humility and patience and courage."

"Courage?"

"Ja, the courage to go back to school each day and face the same situation."

Lisetta tried, but after a month she was tired of being humble, patient, and courageous. It became even harder for her to get up in the morning, and she did her tasks with a gloomy face.

"It's time we had a talk —about Grandma Bech," said Minnie one afternoon when Lisetta returned from school."

"About Grandma Bech?"

"Ja, the winter she was alone on the prairie. Did she ever tell you about it?"

"She just told me that her first husband came to America when she was eighteen."

Minnie sat down in the rocking chair and told Lisetta the story of that winter:

"In 1871, Matthius and Augusta Escher and their baby (your Aunt Hulda) left their village of Althut in Prussia and emigrated to America and then traveled to Illinois. They wanted to homestead, but they had no money to set up farming; so, Matthius worked in a coal mine. After six years, they had saved enough money for homesteading. By that time Matthius had black lung disease from breathing in coal dust, and they had another child (your Uncle Willie) to support; however, they went ahead with their plans and joined a wagon train to Nebraska.

"The wagon train arrived in the spring. Each family chose a parcel of land with a stream on it so that they would have fresh water. The Eschers' land was several miles east from what is now Hoskins.

"The men in the wagon train helped each other to make dugouts to live in while they built a small sod house for each family. The women planted vegetable gardens – potatoes, beets, onions, rutabagas, squash - vegetables that would keep through the winter.

"When winter came, each family had to fend for itself because of the snow, the lack of roads, and the isolation. Staying warm in sub-zero temperatures and strong blustery winds proved impossible for Matthius. In March, he got a chill and a fever that developed into pneumonia, and he was not strong enough to fight to survive. Augusta was left alone with two young children and a baby on the way – your Aunt Anna.

"I'd have been scared to death," interrupted Lisetta. "How did she manage to stay alive?"

"Well, one thing she didn't do was to sit around and feel sorry for herself."

"The first thing she did was to bury her husband. Then she went back into the sod house and decided on a plan: she would make the farm look deserted. The local Pawnees left the homesteaders alone, but the marauding Sioux still roamed the area from time to time. She moved everything she needed for survival into the dugout, leaving enough items in the sod house to make it look like it had been rapidly abandoned. She covered the door of the dugout with branches, and unless you got right up to the dugout, you couldn't see it was there.

"During the daytime, she and the children huddled together under the quilts. When the temperature was bitterly cold, she brought one of the cows into the dugout for warmth. At night, when the smoke couldn't be seen, she made a small fire and fixed hot milk or potato soup. Sometimes at dusk or in the early morning, when the Sioux liked to hunt, she would see them roaming the hills, and she prayed for safety.

"When the children were asleep, she went outside to milk the cows, fetch wood or water, and dig up vegetables. Eventually when the stack of wood had been used up, she collected cow pies to burn. Then the one remaining cow disappeared, and they were without milk. Fortunately, an old Pawnee found the cow and led her back on a rope to the dugout. He must have known for some time that they were there."

"Wow," said Lisetta, overwhelmed.

Minnie continued. "Augusta's worst experience was ahead of her, when Anna was born. Since there was no one to help Augusta. she did what she could to prepare. She brought in cow pies to keep a fire going to boil water, and she kept a knife and a ball of twine handy. Poor little Hulda and Willie had to look on and watch their mother. After the birth, Augusta cut the cord, tied it with twine, cleared Anna's nose and mouth, slapped her to make her cry, washed her, and wrapped her tightly in a blanket. Then she washed herself and collapsed, too exhausted to move. Hulda was left to take care of herself and Willie until the next day.

"By spring, Augusta's strength had returned. One morning as she walked through the melting snow to fetch water from the stream, she heard a horse approaching. She hid among the bushes and watched as a young man led his horse to the stream. It was August Bech, your grandfather. She watched him for a while, and when she thought it was safe, she came out of the bushes. He was so surprised, he almost fell into the stream."

Lisetta laughed.

"Your grandfather wanted a wife, and she needed him, so they soon married. Grandpa Bech's younger half-brother Herman came from Germany twelve years later to homestead, and he fell in love with Hulda and married her. So; mother and daughter married two half-brothers."

"So, what does that make Herman and Hulda's children – my half-half-cousins?"

"I don't know, Zettie. It's all too mixed up for me."

"Well, the story had a happy ending."

"Zettie, do you see why I told you Grandma's story?"

"Ja, I'll stop feeling sorry for myself."

"That's a good girl. And I have a plan, too. I'm going to Wayne to talk with the County Superintendent of Schools. Your grandmother wouldn't have just sat around doing nothing.

*   *   *

A week later, Gus drove Minnie to the county courthouse in Wayne, where they were directed to the office of Superintendent Pearl Sewell. Minnie explained Lisetta's problem with Mrs. Bosen, and the superintendent promised to stop by District 60 School soon and look into the matter. When Pearl Sewell arrived at the school several weeks later, Mrs. Bosen was teaching a lesson. The superintendent waited until the end of the lesson, and then said," I would like to hear Lisetta Meritz read."

Mrs. Bosen flushed, realizing why the superintendent had come. Lisetta took out her reading book, stood up, and read lickity split. When she finished, she remained standing, her eyes flashing with fire.

"Well, Mrs. Bosen," said Superintendent Sewell," I think Lisetta Meritz can be promoted to the sixth grade." Mrs. Bosen nodded, and Lisetta proudly walked over and sat down at a desk in the sixth-grade section. The rest of the school year went smoothly for Lisetta. After a brief period of catching up to the sixth graders, she had no trouble. When sixth grade exams came in May, she was determined to take them even if she was on her deathbed. But no such act of courage was required.

*   *   *

Shortly after school was out, Gus informed Minnie that his cattle were ready to be sold. The market was up; he had not kept his cattle so long this time, but they were fat enough for him to make a substantial profit. Minnie was excited that she could buy a Steinway piano. She imagined the black parlor grand sitting elegantly in her parlor, and she pictured herself and Gus sitting in their parlor in the evenings and listening to the tunes played by Lisetta.

All went well. The cattle sold for a good price, and the music store had a Steinway parlor grand in stock. A week later, the truck pulled into the Meritz lane to deliver the piano. Lisetta and Minnie watched as the tarpaulin-covered behemoth, resting on its side, was wheeled on a dolly up a ramp onto the front steps and rolled through the front door and into the living room. Minnie directed them to a corner opposite the French doors, where visitors would see the piano when they entered the room. From the sofa and chairs around the room, they could watch as Lisetta performed for them.

Minnie had no idea what Lisetta would have to go through in order to perform, but Lisetta began to find out. Minnie enrolled Lisetta and Lyle in the Norfolk Conservatory of Music, taught by the Straven sisters. Lyle took violin lessons from one of the sisters; Lisetta took piano from the other.

At first Lisetta was eager. She wanted to learn how to play simple tunes and songs. But Miss Helen Straven, an excellent musician herself, was not interested in merely teaching tunes. Her

45

pupils would learn scales, triads, arpeggios, intervals, modes, modulations, and Latin musical terms. From her lessons, Lisetta discovered that Miss Straven's predominant traits were perfectionism, orderliness, and stubbornness. Each lesson always began in the same way.

"Let's hear your scales and arpeggios, Lisetta." Lisetta played her G major and G minor scales slowly and almost accurately.

"How much did you practice this week?" Lisetta had practiced a half-hour per day instead of the hour Miss Straven required.

"Did you learn this piece in G major?" Lisetta had worked at it, but evidently not long enough or diligently enough.

"I'll hear that again after you've practiced more. Right now, I want you to analyze this music. Mark each interval in it with a capital M for major and a small m for minor."

Lisetta sat at the piano and stared at the music. After fifteen minutes, she said very quietly, "I don't remember how."

"I've explained the major and minor intervals several times to you, Lisetta. You think about it."

Lisetta sat there and thought until her lesson time was up and Miss Straven had excused her with an admonition to practice.

"What a sourpuss!" said Minnie when Lisetta walked out of the conservatory.

"I hate piano lessons! I'll never learn to play tunes!"

"Patience," said Minnie. "It takes patience."

Chapter 7: Growing Up

During the first Saturday in July, Minnie and Lisetta were busy preparing food for Mission Festival Sunday. It would be a big celebration, with visitors coming from Lutheran churches in Norfolk, Stanton, Hadar, and Winside. There would be a guest preacher for the afternoon service and wonderful food at the noon meal. Minnie would take fried chicken, potato salad, bread, and rhubarb pie.

When the Gus Meritzes arrived at the church for the festival, the street in front of the church and all of the side streets were full of automobiles and buggies. Gus let Minnie out with her basket of food and drove off with Lyle and Lisetta to find a place to park.

"I remember when I was a little boy," he told them, "the Mission Festival was held on the Buss family farm south of Hoskins, in their apple orchard."

Lyle thought this was strange. "An apple orchard! Did you sit in the trees and eat?"

"No, smart ass! We cleared the ground of leaves and branches and put our benches and tables under the trees. Well, times haven't changed so much," said Gus as he parked the car. "We'll be eating outside under the trees again today, unless it rains." He looked at the sky and determined that the clouds were not rain clouds.

When Gus, Lyle and Lisetta reached the church, they saw Minnie motioning to them.

"She wants to show us where she put her food," Gus said. He looked down a long table loaded with fried chicken, sliced ham, potato and Jello salads, and home-baked breads and rolls. On a second long table were all of the cakes: angel food, devil's food, white, lemon, and spice; and all of the pies: apple, peach, rhubarb, raisin, blueberry, custard, chocolate, and lemon.

"I'll try to at least get a piece of your rhubarb pie," Gus said to Minnie, "but I can't promise anything because I'm helping at the concession stand with the lemonade and the ice cream."

The people were already lining up to get their food. Minnie tied on an apron and stood behind the long table to help dish up. Lisetta got in line, filled her plate, and looked around for someone to eat with. She saw her cousin Helen and her Aunt Hannah seated at a table near the concession stand and went to join them. Lisetta did not know them well. Since the death of her husband, Aunt Hannah had become somewhat of a recluse, refusing invitations and limiting her outings to church activities. But Helen, who was about Lisetta's age, attended the parochial school which Lisetta would be entering in the fall, and Lisetta thought they might become good friends.

Following the service, everyone headed for the food tables for a second bite to eat. Then the ladies packed up their baskets as the men took down the tables and benches. By five o'clock, the churchyard was deserted. Instead of going home, Gus drove the automobile south out of Hoskins, rounded a bend in the road, and headed for the Lutheran Cemetery. (Minnie, who had promised her mother that she would keep the mausoleum clean, came here several times a year to sweep it out.) As soon as they entered the cemetery, they could see the red brick mausoleum standing proudly in the center of all the graves. Gus parked on the dirt road, and Minnie headed for the vault. She unlocked the wrought-iron gate and fetched the broom which she kept out of sight around the corner inside the vault. As she swept out the dust and the dried leaves that had blown in, Gus wandered among the graves with Lyle and Lisetta.

He asked them to read the information on the tombstones, and he responded with additional information about each one:

"Gustav Meritz, 1841 – 1920 and Bertha Meritz, 1849 – 1922."

"My father and mother, your grandfather and grandmother. You remember them."

"Ernest Bech, 1894 – 1918"

"His grandfather was Matthias Eckert, the one Grandma Bech buried on the prairie, Aunt Hulda's son. He died in France during the war."

They walked to an older section of the cemetery.

"Wilhelmina Bus, 1842 – 1919."

"That was August Buss's wife – the Buss who had the mission festivals in his orchard."

"Her tombstone has a message on it in German," remarked Lyle.

"Ja. German was the language used in church and school until World War I. Then it was forbidden by the government to even speak the language in public. We had to learn English fast."

Minnie joined them.

"Gus, what are you doing amongst these old tombstones?" she asked.

"Giving Lyle and Lisetta a history lesson."

As they headed back to the car past the mausoleum, Gus couldn't help comparing the humble graves they had just been examining with the Bech vault.

"Your father was certainly a proud man, Minnie. In life and in death."

"And a bit of an ornery cuss," added Minnie. "He always wanted his way, but Ma outsmarted him sometimes. I remember once when she gave me a bowl of butter for a poor, old neighbor lady. She said, *"Minnie, go through the trees so your father doesn't see you. He doesn't believe in charity, and we don't want to get him angry."*

"He sure was an ornery cuss," repeated Gus.

Minnie continued, "Before my father died, he had this mausoleum built and made Ma promise to keep it swept out, and then before she died, she turned the promise over to me."

"So, his humility continues," said Gus sarcastically.

* * *

At the end of the summer, shortly after Lisetta's eleventh birthday, she started parochial school in Hoskins. She was just as frightened on her first day there as she had been six years earlier at District 60. She knew that she would need real courage ahead. All summer long she had been hearing from Lyle about the teacher, Mr. Mulbrecht. Last year had been Lyle's first year at Trinity Evangelical Lutheran School and Mr. Mulbrecht's, too. Mr. Mulbrecht was very strict, partly from the need to establish a reputation at a new school and partly because of his nature and his beliefs. By nature, he was a sober man, lacking in humor, and an earnest man, determined to do the right thing. He believed that children were born evil and that it was his duty to punish and repress the evil nature in each of his pupils so that good could develop. Lisetta was afraid of Mr. Mulbrecht because of his sober appearance (he always wore the same black suit with a stiffly starched white shirt and a black tie) and because he was a man. She had never had a male teacher before, and Mr. Mulbrecht was nothing like Gus, the man she most admired.

On the first day of school, Mr. Mulbrecht seated the older students by confirmation class: those who would be confirmed in the spring and those who would be confirmed the following spring. He seated the younger students by grade levels. Lisetta found herself near the back of the class, with Rose Lenser and Helen Meritz across the aisle. Earl Muller was directly behind Lisetta. At country school, the teachers had never placed Earl in back of any of the girls because they knew how he loved to tease them. But Mr. Mulbrecht did not take inherent nature into account when he seated his pupils. To him, there were only two natures, evil and good, and all were evil until he had had a chance to change them. After seating the pupils, Mr. Mulbrecht established the rules for behavior: no talking or whispering to classmates; no daydreaming; no wasting time; no distracting behavior; no impoliteness or rudeness; no going to the outhouse except at recess or lunch time.

For the first two months, Lisetta kept all of the rules. When Earl Muller squeezed her shoulder hard each time he walked past her to the teacher's desk, she ignored him. And when he dipped her pigtail in his inkwell, she resisted the temptation to write him a nasty note. She sat quietly and watched Mr. Mulbrecht as he kept discipline in the classroom. He never raised his voice; he never threatened to punish bad behavior; his discipline was direct and without warning.

Lisetta noticed that he seemed to enjoy sneaking up behind a pupil who was misbehaving and then digging his fingers in under the collarbone until the offender slunk down in pain. For a severe punishment, he administered a sharp, unexpected blow to the side of the head. More than once, she had seen him slap Earl when he was about to bother her.

Lisetta didn't manage to stay out of trouble forever. One day she forgot to go to the outhouse during morning recess. Because of Mr. Mulbrecht's rule about leaving the classroom, she was afraid to inform him of the emergency. She tried her best to wait until noon recess, shifting this way and that in her seat, but to no avail. The accident happened, and Lisetta prayed that she would not be called up to put an arithmetic problem on the board. She knew the rule about disturbing others, but she had no choice. She wrote a note and passed it to her cousin, Helen, explaining her situation. Helen wrote back, "Come to my house at lunch. You can change into some of my clothes." At lunchtime, Lisetta waited until the classroom was empty. Then she cleaned up the area the best she could and walked across the street to Helen's house, where her Aunt Hannah greeted her warmly and gave her a change of clothes.

Lisetta and Helen had gotten away with passing a note back and forth. This experience emboldened Lisetta. A week later, she wrote a note to Rose, folded it up, and put out her hand to pass it. Suddenly she felt a sharp pain under her collarbone. Mr. Mulbrecht! She winced and slunk down in her seat. Mr. Mulbrecht passed quietly by and headed back to the front of the room.

At the end of six weeks, Lisetta received her first report card, which included a numerical score in reading, physiology, penmanship, orthography, mental arithmetic, history, grammar, arithmetic, drawing, religion, German, and deportment. She was surprised that she had studied so many different subjects. A few of her scores were in the nineties; five were in the eighties; four in the seventies; and one, arithmetic, was sixty-five. Since Lisetta had always thought of herself as smart, especially in arithmetic, her report card was a blow to her ego.

When she got home, she sheepishly handed her report card to Minnie, who looked it over carefully. Minnie first studied the picture of a country school on the front of the card. Underneath the picture were the words: Model Rural School. At the bottom of the card was a slogan: *If you wish to succeed in this life, be faithful, be cautious, be industrious, be neat, be honest, be just, be kind, be true, be courteous.* When she opened the card, she saw all of Lisetta's grades recorded in neat columns.

"Your grade in religion is good," Minnie said, "and grammar. But a 65 in arithmetic? I thought that arithmetic was your favorite subject."

"It is, Ma. But parochial school is harder than country school."

"Then you need to work harder," responded Minnie.

Minnie looked over the rest of the card. At the bottom of the inside page was another slogan, which she drew to Gus's attention. "Here's a good message for you, Gus: *The young man who smokes cigarettes need not worry about the future; he has none.*"

"That doesn't apply to me," answered Gus. "I smoke cigars, and I'm not a young man anymore."

Minnie turned over the card and looked at the back page. There was a place for the parent's signature, and at the bottom of the page, a quote from Abraham Lincoln: *The best citizen is he who obeys the mandates of the schoolroom and applies his knowledge to the betterment of mankind.*

"What does the word *mandates* mean?" Minnie asked Lisetta.

"I don't know, Ma. We haven't studied that yet."

"Well, ask Mr. Mulbrecht what it means."

"Yes, Ma." But Lisetta had no intention of asking Mr. Mulbrecht anything. Nor did she complain about him to Minnie. Minnie had gone to bat for her with Mrs. Bosen, but Lisetta felt that her mother would be no match for Mr. Mulbrecht.

*   *   *

In the fall of the following year, Lisetta's class began their confirmation studies. Each day included instruction in German print and script, which again were allowed in churches and schools at the end of World War I. There were weekly classes in Catechism and Bible instruction, both conducted by Pastor Brenner. He assigned some passages to be memorized, some to be paraphrased, others to be summarized, all requiring hard work and careful thought. The nine confirmands worked diligently to prepare for confirmation on Palm Sunday.

In anticipation of this occasion, Minnie had asked Ruth Fletcher, who had made Lisetta's little blue crepe de chine dress, to sew a special dress for her. Minnie and Lisetta looked through a stack of Ruth's patterns and chose one showing a calf-length dress with a loose bodice, a round neckline, three rows of accordion pleats around the skirt, and a narrow row of pleats around the short sleeves. Ruth brought out some samples of materials, and Minnie selected a heavy white silk.

"How will you wear your hair?" Ruth asked Lisetta.

"Like this," Lisetta motioned, "in a braid down the back."

"Then I'll make a pretty big bow out of the left-over silk to dress up your hair."

Ruth had the dress ready a week before Palm Sunday. Minnie and Lisetta picked it up and took the train to Norfolk to shop for stockings and shoes.

On Confirmation Day, Lisetta didn't need to be called to get out of bed. She had been awake for some time, too excited to sleep. She had her breakfast, helped clear up the dishes, and then began to dress for the day: first the long white cotton stockings, then the black patent leather shoes with a single strap across the foot, then the slip, the silk dress; and finally, the beautiful big bow. She examined herself in the mirror. For once, she was satisfied with her reflection.

When the Meritzes arrived at the church, Lisetta took her place in the procession. As the organist played the introduction to "All Glory, Laud, and Honor," Lisetta and her classmates processed in and seated themselves in the front pew that had been reserved for them. Following the sermon and the collection of the offerings, Pastor Brenner invited the confirmands into the chancel for the examination. They stood in a single line, facing the congregation. First came the questions on Luther's *Small Catechism,* followed by recitations from *The Bible,* and finally the rite of confirmation. Then each confirmand knelt at the altar to receive a blessing and a special Biblical verse. As Lisetta knelt, the pastor recited Psalm 37:5, "Commit thy way unto the Lord. Trust also in Him, and He shall bring it to pass." Lisetta wondered what God would someday bring to pass for her.

When confirmation was over, the Gus Meritz family left immediately for home. Minnie wanted to be there to greet their dinner guests. Upon reaching the farm, she donned an apron, peeked at the huge roast in the oven, and checked her table to see that she had not forgotten anything. Not long after, relatives and friends began to arrive. The party was lively. Gus passed around glasses of sweet wine before dinner and offered a toast to Lisetta: "To Zettie, who is a young lady today." Lisetta blushed. She had performed in church, but she preferred to fade into the background now.

Late in the afternoon, when the guests had left, Gus turned to Minnie and said, "Well, Minnie, in talking with the men this afternoon, I've decided to get a new automobile."

"What's wrong with our old one?"

"There's nothing wrong with it, but the new Buicks are much nicer and more convenient. They have glass windows instead of Eisen-glass curtains; you don't have to keep putting the top on and taking if off; and you don't have to crank the automobile to get it started. Besides they're easier to steer. Even you could learn how to drive it, Minnie."

"Well, Gus, maybe I will."

"What? Was that another Minnie who said, *Horses are good enough for me*?"

Within a few weeks, Gus had purchased a new four-door black Buick sedan with black leather upholstery. By the end of the month, he had taught Minnie how to drive. At first, she only drove around the farmyard and up and down the lane. Then she ventured alone into Hoskins to go to the grocery store or to the post office. By the end of the summer, she was ready to drive by herself all the way to Norfolk.

Gus was happy. *If anything happens to me,* he thought, *Minnie will be able to get around.* He was pleased that she could take Lyle and Lisetta into Norfolk when high school started in the fall. During the past year, Gus had been driving Lyle into Norfolk on Sunday afternoon and driving back again on the following Friday afternoon to bring him home from the Ed Meritzes where Lyle had boarded during the school week.

"The house will be empty this year when Lyle and Zettie are both gone during the week," Gus said to Minnie when he returned home.

"For me more than for you, Gus. You're such a gadabout these days."

"What good does it do to make money, Minnie, if you can't take time to enjoy a little of it?"

"Na ja," said Minnie, "a little here, a little there, and soon it's all gone."

*   *   *

When the summer was over, Lisetta joined Lyle as a part of the Ed Meriitz family. Lyle had been sleeping in Aunt Ella's sewing room, just off the landing. Aunt Ella had brought a bed into the room, and while Lyle was in class, she still used the room whenever she had sewing to do. With windows on three sides of the room, it became light early in the morning, but Lyle, who had been used to rising early to milk the cows, did not mind. Engie made room for Lisetta in her room.

A few days before school was to start, Loretta and Lyle took Engie and Lisetta to register for their freshman classes. The four Meritzes went out the back door of the home, walked down an alley to the street behind the house, crossed the street, and walked up the sidewalk towards the front entrance of the school.

As they approached the building, Lisetta was impressed with its architecture. The three-story brick building, built in 1921, had inserts of stone masonry around the windows, the door, along the roof, and at the corners of the building. Ornate carvings graced the triangular stone insert above the main entrance and along the top of the building, and the two tall stone columns on either side of the entrance added a touch of Grecian elegance. A spacious green lawn surrounded three sides of the building and extended in length from one street to another.

Inside the entrance, Lyle pointed out an eight-foot stone statue of a man on a four-foot square pedestal. The figure stood at ease with one leg relaxed and slightly in front of the other, and with one arm down, the other raised and resting on his chest.

"That's Abraham Lincoln," said Lisetta, who had seen his picture in one of the history books at parochial school.

Lyle and Loretta led Engie and Lisetta to the Principal's Office on the first floor and waited for them to register. As freshmen, they had little choice in classes. They both registered for English, civics, algebra, science, Latin, and physical education. For the remaining two periods of the day, they had a choice between electives, such as glee club, orchestra, band, journalism, art, or study hall. Lisetta and Engie both chose study hall so they would not have so much homework to do after school.

When they had finished registering, Lyle and Loretta led them to their lockers, their classrooms, the gymnasium in the basement, and the convocation hall. They climbed to the third floor and entered the balcony, which was filled with rows of seats at different levels. Lyle led them down the steps so that they could peek over the brass railing to the floor two stories below, where there were more rows of seats, all with red horsehair upholstery. Each of the three sections faced a large stage. "This is where we come for our convocations," Lyle informed them.

After the excitement of the first few days of high school, Lisetta settled into the routine of school-home-church. On Sundays, the Gus Meritzes attended church in Hoskins. In the afternoon, Gus and Minnie drove Lyle and Lisetta to the Ed Meritz residence. Minnie never came empty-handed. She brought with her eggs, fresh butter, fresh or canned fruits and vegetables, and a chicken plucked and ready for frying or a chunk of beef or ham or a smoked sausage. She never brought freshly baked bread or pie or cake because Ella was proud of her own baked goods and would have considered this an insult.

During the week, the four young Meritzes followed a strict regimen. At exactly six-thirty in the morning, they sat down to eat their breakfast. At a quarter to eight, they left the house and walked together through the alley to the school. After school, they worked on homework from three-fifteen until four-fifteen. From four-fifteen until dinner at six o'clock, they practiced music: piano for the girls, violin for Lyle. The evenings were filled with more homework or card games. At nine o'clock the young people began getting ready for bed. Each one had to get in and out of the white sparkling bathroom without disturbing its pristine appearance.

On Friday afternoons, Minnie drove into Norfolk to get Lyle and Lisetta and bring them home. Leaving each Friday afternoon meant that they missed all of the school games, the programs, and the dances. Consequently, Lisetta and Lyle didn't have much opportunity to get to know their classmates outside of the classroom. On Saturdays, Lyle and Lisetta helped at the farm in the morning. In the afternoon, Minnie drove them into Norfolk for their music lessons. Afterwards they accompanied her as she did some shopping or ran errands. Then they headed back home for supper. Suppertime on Saturdays was the best time for the Gus Meritz family to visit.

"How was school this week?" Gus asked.

"It's the same every week," answered Lisetta. "The same old routine."

"Routines are good," said Minnie. They bring order into your life and help you to get a lot done. And that can make you feel good about yourself and can make others happy, too."

"Give us an example of that, Minnie," prompted Gus.

"Well, every morning I get up at five o'clock and go out to milk the cows. And I feel good when I can bring in fresh milk and cream for our breakfast at six o'clock. And you enjoy the milk and cream, Gus."

"Actually, I enjoy sleeping in the morning. I could do without your routine in the morning, Minnie."

"Routine, schmootrine! You're just lazy in the morning, Gus."

"Well, you're ambitious enough for both of us, Minnie."

Chapter 8: Gus

With both Lyle and Lisetta gone during the week, Gus needed to fill his days even more with the companionship of friends. On a Friday morning in late March, 1926, Gus headed for Hoskins to see his friend, Milo Hansen, the station master. His mission would be both pleasure and business. He intended to ship a load of cattle by train to Chicago. Lately Gus had been shipping his cattle by train instead of by truck to Omaha because he dealt with larger numbers these days, and it was cheaper to send a large load of cattle directly to Chicago than to pay the truckers to transport them to Omaha. Then, too, Chicago was the center of the meat-packing industry, and unless the market suddenly dropped, he could be assured of a better price for his cattle in Chicago.

When Gus shipped cattle by freight train, he always accompanied them so that he could oversee the care of his animals en route. Also, he liked to be there when they were auctioned off. During the trip, he rode in the caboose of the train, which was comfortable enough, but lonely and tedious. With the train stopping at every station along the way, the trip always took several days and a night. This time, however, Gus planned to invite a friend along for company.

When Gus arrived at the depot, he made arrangements with Milo to ship his cattle on Monday.

"I'll need a ticket for the caboose, too," Gus said.

"You know you can ride free, Gus, when you ship cattle."

"I know, but this time I'm planning to bring along a friend for company."

By the time they had finished their transaction, several men had gathered at a table in the waiting room, and Gus and Milo joined them for a game of poker. The game was interrupted now and then when a train pulled into the depot or a passenger purchased a ticket from Milo or baggage or freight needed to be loaded or unloaded. During these breaks, the men talked and smoked.

Gus headed back to the farm in the late afternoon. *Life is sweet*, he thought, as he drove along. He had enjoyed his afternoon with his friends and was looking forward to the weekend with Lyle and Lisetta at home. After supper, Gus asked them if they wanted to go with him for a brief visit to the Getzmers. Lyle had other plans, but Lisetta was eager to go. When they reached the Getzmer house, Emelia answered their knock. She invited them into the dining room, where Wilhelm was seated at the table.

While the two men discussed the trip to Chicago, Lisetta watched Walter in the kitchen as he stood at the kitchen sink and washed his face, brushed his teeth, and combed his hair. When he finished, he passed through the dining room on his way upstairs, but did not stop to visit.

On his way home, Gus said, "It's been a good day, Zettie." Lisetta nodded.

"So, Mr. Getzmer said *Yes*?"

"Ja, it's a good time of the year for him. We'll stay a few days, and while he's visiting his brother Herman, I'll visit my brother – your Uncle Willie."

On Monday morning before the sun was up, truckers came out to the farm, loaded up the cattle, and took them to the depot. Minnie had packed Gus's suitcase the night before. Just before leaving the house, Gus surreptitiously slipped into his suitcase a deck of cards and a quart of whiskey. Minnie drove Gus to the Getzmer farm to pick up Wilhelm and then drove them to the station. She was in a hurry to get back to her chores and did not come into the depot. "Pick us up on Saturday, about eight o'clock in the evening," Gus reminded her.

Gus and Wilhelm took their suitcases with them into the caboose and seated themselves for the journey. While they were waiting for the train to leave the station, Gus pulled two cigars out of the inside pocket of his suit coat and offered one to Wilhelm. When the train pulled out, the sun was just peeking over the eastern horizon. As dawn turned into day, the hills changed from gray to gray-green and finally to emerald-green. The melting of the winter snows had left the ground soaked with moisture, and these earliest spring meadows were the lushest of the season.

"Ich liebe Fruhling," said Wilhelm, in appreciation of the beauty around him."

"Ich liebe Sommer, Herbst, Winter und Fruhling," answered Gus.

"Ja, Gus, du liebst alle und alles."

Switching to English, Gus said, "I have a surprise for you." As he unzipped his suitcase, a strong smell of whiskey engulfed the caboose. "Well, I hope my clothes enjoyed that whiskey," Gus said, "but don't say anything about this to Minnie."

In spite of the absence of whiskey, the two friends enjoyed their games of Schafskopf between naps and visiting about friends and neighbors. Wilhelm was looking forward to meeting Tillie, Hank's bride, and seeing Mabel and Dick again, who had recently moved to Chicago. Gus listened attentively to the Getzmer news, but the drone of the wheels eventually overcame him, and he fell fast asleep in an upright position.

Gus had a strange dream. He was all alone in the dark, walking towards a light which was way off in the distance. From the direction opposite the light, he could hear Minnie's voice calling, "Gus, Gus, don't go! Come back!" Gus turned around and tried to go back in the direction of Minnie's voice, but his legs would not move. And then, suddenly a train picked him up and carried him towards the light. Another train passed by, going in the opposite direction. He could see clearly all of the passengers on the train; all of them were strangers, except for Wilhelm Getzmer. The freight train came to a stop, and Gus awoke.

"You were in my dream," he said to Wilhelm. "It was a strange dream. I didn't understand it." Gus relayed the dream to Wilhelm as they had their breakfast in the lunch room adjacent to the depot.

"I don't understand it either," said Wilhelm, "except for zeh train."

"Ja, but you were on one train and I was on another, and we were headed in opposite directions."

"Ich weiss nicht," said Wilhelm. "Maybe vee each take a long trip alone. I vant to go back to Deutschland before I die."

"Well, you can't take a train to Germany – unless they've built tracks across the ocean."

"Nein, but I take a train to zeh ship."

"Well, maybe I'll take the train to Idaho one of these days to see my brother Max. It would probably be safer than if I drove."

"Ja, ja. Minnie vould agree."

*   *   * a

A year later, Gus's dream began to come true. Gus developed a cough, not just a little cough, but a deep, hacking cough. When the cough was still with him a month later, Minnie said, "I don't like the sound of that cough, Gus. I think you should go see the doctor."

"No, Minnie. It came by itself, and it will go away alone."

But the cough did not go away – not in April or May. Finally in June, when Gus was tired of coughing, in fact, tired most of the time, he went to see a doctor in Norfolk. Gus went alone one morning. When he returned, he had no explanation for his cough, but the doctor had not liked the sound of his right lung and had scheduled an appointment at The Campbell Clinic on Norfolk Avenue. This time Minnie went with him. At the clinic, Gus had a series of x-rays. While Minnie and Gus sat in silence in the waiting room, Doctor Campbell studied the x-rays and then called them into his office.

"It's not good, Mr. Meritz. There is a large shadow on your right lung."

"What does that mean?" asked Minnie.

"It looks like cancer. Are you in pain, Gus?"

"No. Only the cough"

"Do you cough up blood?"

"No, no blood."

"As it progresses, there will be blood and pain, I'm afraid."

"Is there no hope?" asked Minnie.

58

"Medicine hasn't found a cure for cancer yet, but I wouldn't give up hope." He turned to Gus.

"I want you to come to the clinic once a month for an x-ray so we can track this."

*   *   *

At first Gus and Minnie said nothing about the cancer to Lyle and Lisetta or to other relatives and friends. *Perhaps,* they thought, *a miracle would happen, and the cancer would go away.* During the summer, Gus got thinner and thinner. But his appetite was good; it seemed like he was always hungry. Minnie's food had never tasted so delicious. By the end of the summer, however, he could not eat enough to keep up his strength.

"When are you going to get better, Dad?" Lisetta asked one day in August, a week before her fifteenth birthday.

"It looks like I'm not, Zettie." Lisetta knew in her heart that this was true, but she said, "Yes, you will, Dad. You'll see."

*   *   *

In early September, Minnie scheduled a family portrait with a photographer in Norfolk. She wanted a remembrance of her family before Gus became bedridden. For the occasion, she wore her best black dress and her gold beads; Gus and Lyle were attired in black suits and bow ties; Lisetta chose the new dress and the pearls her parents had given her for her birthday. When the pictures had been developed, Lyle and Lisetta discussed them.

"Dad still looks handsome, don't you think?" asked Lisetta.

"Ja, but Ma looks awfully strained and worried."

*   *   *

By October, Gus was bedridden. He no longer went to Norfolk to see Doctor Campbell. Instead, Doctor Campbell came out to the farm to see him, to bring him pain medication and to check his pulse and lungs. Minnie always stood by while Doctor Campbell checked Gus, and when he had finished, she always offered him something to eat, and the doctor always declined.

Gus was concerned for Minnie. He felt that she needed help with the operation of the farms. "Maybe Lyle and Lisetta should come home to help out," he suggested. But Minnie was not in favor of having their education disrupted.

"I can manage the farms," Minnie said. "I'll hire a housekeeper to do the housework and the cooking, and I'll oversee the hired men."

"That's good, Minnie. That will get you out of the house, too. You don't want to spend all of your time around a sick bed."

Minnie hired Ida Hintz, a relative of the Getzmers, to housekeep. Ida moved into the bedroom that had been Gus and Minnie's. Minnie had the hired men move some of the dining room furniture into the living room and then move two beds into the dining room, one for Gus and a second bed for herself. She wanted to be near Gus at night without disturbing him. She had Gus's bed placed next to a window and opposite the kitchen door. From this position, he could either watch the activity outside or the activity in the kitchen, which was the hub of the household.

*   *   *

Early in November, during one of Doctor Campbell's house calls, he told Gus and Minnie about a new operation on cancer patients that Doctor Hedbloom in Chicago was performing.

"I've talked with him," he said, "and he's willing to take you, Gus."

"I don't know how we could manage the trip," Minnie said. "Gus is too sick to make the journey alone, and I've never been farther from here than Omaha."

"Don't worry," said Doctor Campbell. "I'll make all of the arrangements. I'll find you a place to stay while Gus is in the hospital, and I'll go with you on the train."

*   *   *

A week later, an ambulance came out to the farm to get Gus. Minnie stepped into the back of the ambulance and rode with him on the way to the station. When they got there, Milo Hansen was waiting to help his old friend onto the train. The bed was wheeled into a special compartment which Doctor Campbell had arranged for Gus and Minnie, and the doctor took an adjacent compartment for himself.

"Well," Gus said to Minnie, "I'm finally getting you to go to Chicago with me."

"Shush," said Minnie. "None of your foolishness."

At the Chicago end of the line, Doctor Campbell had arranged for another ambulance to pick up Gus from the depot and carry him to the hospital. Again, Minnie rode in the back of the ambulance. When Gus was situated in the hospital, Doctor Campbell took Minnie in a taxicab to a residence nearby.

Before Doctor Hedbloom operated, he ordered numerous x-rays of Gus's lungs and his heart. He found that the right lung was collapsed and that the heart was enlarged from the strain of decreased oxygen. Since Gus's heart would be unable to withstand a general anesthetic, the doctor would have to operate with one local to the area.

Minnie was not allowed into the operating room, but the operation was described to her later. First, they strapped Gus's arms and legs to the operating table so that he could not flail about. Then they anesthetized the area around the right lung with needles. Next, they made an incision in the right side, separated the ribs surrounding the lung, inserted radium sticks into the lung, and then eased the ribs back into place and closed the incision. Throughout all of this, Minnie was told, Gus did not cry aloud; but he had writhed in so much pain, that by the end of the operation, he had rubbed all of the skin off his elbows.

Gus stayed in the hospital in Chicago for three weeks. Doctor Campbell had gone home, but he had made arrangements for their return trip and had an ambulance waiting for them when they arrived in Norfolk. From the depot, Gus was taken to the hospital in Norfolk to complete his recuperation from the surgery. While Gus was in the hospital, Minnie wrote to his brother Max in Idaho, informing him of the seriousness of Gus's condition.

*   *   *

By mid-December, Gus had shown no improvement.

> "He might as well go home," Doctor Campbell told Minnie. "However, he'll need a full-time nurse. I've arranged for Miss Hilgreth to join your household. She will bathe him, give him his hypos, and assist me when I come out to aspirate the blood and pus from Gus's lung."

The night before Gus came home from the hospital, Minnie was awakened by an eerie sound: "Whoo, whoo, whoooooo." *Is it a turtle dove,* she wondered, but decided that it was too spooky a sound for one of their barn birds. (If Minnie had stepped outside, she would have seen that an owl had found a perch in the corner support of the front porch.)

Lyle and Lisetta were happy to have their father home for Christmas. They knew that this was his last Christmas, and they were anxious to be near him. Gus did his best to cheer them all up. He slept much of the time, but when he was awake, he still managed to tease them from time to time.

> "Dad never complains," Lisetta said to Minnie one day. "Isn't he in pain?"

> "He's in a great deal of pain. I hear him moaning at night in his sleep. The moaning and that verdammte owl keep me awake most of the night."

> "I hear that owl, too, Ma. It's funny how it chose our porch just at this time."

> "Mark my words, Zettie. It's a bad omen."

Sometimes in the middle of the night, Lisetta awoke to the owl's hooting, and then she heard her mother stirring down below. Gus's appetite was usually poor now. But in the middle of the night, he sometimes got a terrible craving for one of Minnie's dishes, like her fruit soup, and she got up and fixed it for him.

61

When school began again after the Christmas holidays, Lisetta felt almost more at home at Aunt Ella's house than she had in her own home, which was so full of strangers now. There were the housekeeper and the nurse and the extra farm help. Gus had so many visitors: Doctor Campbell, Pastor Brenner, Mr. Getzmer among others. In January, her Uncle Max from Idaho was added to the household. He had gotten Minnie's letter and had decided to come and stay through the winter or until Gus tired of him. He was one visitor whom Lisetta enjoyed having around. In fact, he was good for them all. He played cards with Gus, listened to Minnie's farm problems and gave her advice, and was a companion to Lyle and Lisetta. Max stayed until the middle of March, when he was needed back home for the spring planting. When he said good-bye at the depot, Minnie's heart was full of gratitude as she handed him a basket of her Kaffeekuchen. Then she turned around quickly so that he would not see her tears.

Several weeks after Max left, Lyle became ill with a high fever, a headache, and nausea. A day later, Lisetta complained of backache and nausea and began to vomit. When Doctor Campbell came to see Gus, Minnie asked him to go upstairs and examine her children.

> "Smallpox," he announced when he returned downstairs. "You'll need to quarantine the house. No visitors. Try to keep everyone except Miss Hilgreth away from Gus. He must not get this!"

For a week, only Miss Hilgreth went in and out of Gus's room. But it was no use. Gus developed a severe headache and a high fever. Then he became delirious. Minnie begged Miss Hilgreth to let her see Gus, but the nurse stubbornly refused to disobey the doctor's orders.

> "Just look after your children," she said. "There's nothing you can do for Gus."

Oh yes, there is, thought Minnie. She went into the living room and sat on the sofa, her head in her hands, and prayed.

The next day Gus's fever was down, and his mind was clear. His face was covered with red spots, the outward sign of the smallpox. These turned into pustules, the pustules became scabs, and the scabs finally dropped off. Gus had miraculously survived the smallpox. He was overjoyed that Lyle and Lisetta had escaped death and that Minnie had not contracted the disease. He felt good enough for company.

> "Send word to Herr Getzmer that he can come to visit again," he said to Minnie.

Throughout the remainder of April, Wilhelm came every day to visit Gus. But the time was short. Wilhelm had already made plans for a trip to Germany in May. However, he put off telling Gus about the trip as long as he could. Eventually, he could postpone it no longer. The day before he left for New York by train, he broke the news to Gus. Gus was dismayed.

> "Don't go, Herr Getzmer. I'll never see you again."

> "I've got to go, Gus. I'm not young anymore. If I don't go now, I'll never go."

"Don't go," begged Gus.

"Nein. Ich muss gehen." Gus did not ask a third time.

"Now I understand that dream on the way to Chicago. You're taking the train to New York, and I'm taking the train to the promised land."

"Nein, nein, Gus. It's not good-bye. It's Auf Wiedersehen."

"No, not this time." Gus tried hard to smile. "Be good! I want to play Schafskopf with you in heaven someday."

Gus turned his head away so that Wilhelm would not see his tears. Wilhelm squeezed his hand tightly, let loose, and walked out of the room.

Gus remained almost lifeless for several weeks. Then he rallied at the weekend when Lyle and Lisetta came home. "Dad looks better, Ma. There's a bloom on his cheeks," observed Lyle.

"Ja, he took a bad turn when Mr. Getzmer left for Germany, but he's back to his old cheerful nature again."

"Is there anything I can do, Ma?" asked Lisetta.

"Ja, Zettie. Your father's toenails and fingernails need cutting. Get the scissors and cut them for him." Lisetta got the scissors and walked into the dining room.

"Time to cut your nails, Dad."

"Hello, my Liebchen! Do you think you're old enough to handle a pair of scissors?"

Lisetta smiled and began to carefully cut his nails. Gus lay quietly while she worked. By the time she had finished, he had fallen asleep.

Gus awakened about suppertime and watched the family eating in the kitchen. He was not hungry, but Minnie coaxed him to take a few spoonsful of broth. After supper, they listened to the radio for a while in the dining room. Lisetta was tired; so, she said good-night early and went upstairs to bed.

About two o'clock in the morning, she was awakened by the "Who, who, whooo," of the owl. Then she heard her mother's voice: "Lyle, Zettie, come down! I think your father is dying."

Sometime during the night, Gus had lost consciousness. Now he was taking long, deep breaths with occasional lapses between. Minnie, Lyle and Lisetta stood around the bed while the breaths became more and more shallow and finally stopped. The clock struck three. They just stood there for a while. Then Lisetta said, "I didn't get to say good-bye to him."

"You didn't need to, Zettie. He knew you loved him."

"Are you all right, Ma?" asked Lyle.

"Ja, but leave me alone with your father just now."

"Come on, Zettie." Lyle led her out onto the front porch. He turned on the porch light, and they both looked for the owl in the corner. It was gone.

*   *   *

On Sunday, Minnie, Lyle, and Lisetta did not attend church in the morning, nor did they go to Lyle's baccalaureate service in the afternoon. Early in the afternoon, Pastor Brenner came out to the farm to plan the funeral with Minnie. It would take place on Wednesday afternoon, the sixteenth of May. There would be an open casket, as was the custom. Pastor Brenner gave Minnie a list of all the arrangements she would need to make: contacting a funeral parlor, selecting a casket, choosing the pallbearers, ordering flowers, purchasing a headstone, and informing relatives and friends. Minnie was glad that she had two children to help her with these duties.

After Pastor Brenner had left, Minnie called a funeral parlor in Norfolk and made arrangements for them to come for Gus's body on Monday morning. In the afternoon, she planned to drive to Norfolk to select the casket and make the other arrangements.

The following day, the sky was overcast with high gray clouds. Minnie, Lyle, and Lisetta stood on the porch, waiting for the hearse to arrive.

"I didn't hear the owl last night," Lisetta said.

"I told you he was a bad omen. He was just waiting for your father to die."

"Perhaps he was off hunting," said Lyle.

"No, mark my words. His eerie mission is over. He won't be back."

"Here it comes," said Lyle. They looked up and saw a cloud of dust on the road, and then the long, black hearse turning into the lane.

"Bring them into the dining room," Minnie instructed Lyle as she went in for a final look at Gus.

The men from the funeral parlor opened up the back door of the hearse, removed a long wooden box, and carried it into the dining room. They lifted the body into the box and closed the lid. As they carried out the box, Minnie followed behind with Gus's clothes. They slid the box into the back and laid the clothes on top of the box.

"I'm worried about his appearance," Minnie said. "His cheeks are so sunken in."

"We can put cotton inside his mouth to plump out his cheeks," said one of the men. "Don't worry, Mrs. Meritz. He'll look just fine."

Just fine, thought Lisetta. *To look just fine he would need to be alive.* Lisetta stood looking in at the box through the window of the hearse. The driver waited a moment and then pulled away very slowly, sensitive to the feelings of the bystanders. The three watched as the hearse drove up the lane, turned the corner, and climbed the hill of the main road. Then they lost sight of it as it went over the hill.

An hour later they left for Norfolk to make the funeral arrangements. Their first stop was the funeral parlor. The funeral director showed them into a room with display caskets. Minnie selected one of the more expensive ones – a bronze casket with a delicate ivory-colored velvet interior.

"It's so expensive!" Lyle said.

"Ja, but I don't want anything cheap for your father."

"Of course not," said the funeral director. "Now, then, Mrs. Meritz, let's sit down and decide who you want for your pallbearers. You'll need six strong men."

Minnie talked it over with Lyle and Lisetta and decided on four of Gus's special friends and two of the Getzmer boys, Bill and Paul. (She would have liked to include Hank, but Chicago was too far away.)

Minnie and Gus already had their burial plots at Prospect Hill Cemetery, but Minnie needed to choose a headstone for Gus, which she did at her next stop – a large granite stone, four feet tall and six feet wide. The engraving would read: *Gustave Julius Meritz, 1883 – 1928.*

Their last stop was the florist's.

"Do you have any suggestions for our flowers?" Minnie asked the florist.

"The wife usually selects a bouquet to be placed on the casket when it is closed. Roses are commonly used. Is there a flower which was special in your marriage?"

"Ja, I carried a bouquet of white carnations, vines, and tiny pink rosebuds when I married my husband in 1907."

"Good. We'll make it a beautiful large bouquet of white carnations and pink rosebuds, and I'll add a few ivy streamers."

"Now from the son and daughter?" asked the florist.

"How about red roses?" asked Lyle.

"With blue forget-me-nots," added Lisetta.

"Fine. Forget-me-nots are blooming right now, and red roses, of course, are always available in the florist trade."

When the three arrived home from their trip to Norfolk, the house seemed empty. Minnie had already discharged the nurse and the housekeeper, and there weren't any visitors hovering about. Gus's empty bed was still in the dining room.

"Do you want me to take Dad's bed down?" Lyle asked Minnie.

"Not today. Let's do it tomorrow morning. We'll need the table back in the dining room when people come to view the body. I thought we'd put the casket in the living room. People can go in there first and then come into the dining room for some food."

The next day at noontime, the casket was brought back from the funeral parlor. Minnie, Lyle, and Lisetta had a private viewing time before friends and relatives came to pay their respects at three o'clock. When Minnie saw Gus, she was happy that the cotton had worked. His cheeks did not look like two cavities anymore. His suit, shirt, and tie looked attractive, and his hair had been shampooed.

"Come here," Minnie said and motioned to Lisetta. "How does your father look?"

Lisetta looked at her father lying there, his hands folded on his chest, his gold wedding band on his finger. His skin looked white, bloodless. His eyes were closed, but his mouth seemed right, just turned up slightly at the corners, suggesting a hint of smile.

*   *   *

On the day of the funeral, the hearse came out first to get the coffin and take it to the church. Then it came back to get Minnie, Lyle, and Lisetta. Once again, they waited on the front porch and watched as the vehicle came down the lane. As the three entered the hearse, they reminded Lisetta of three crows, each dressed in black from head to foot.

When the hearse turned off the main street in Hoskins and into the side street where the church was located, they noticed that people were already sitting on chairs in the front yard of the church.

"Why are all of those people sitting outside the church?" Minnie asked.

"Waiting for the funeral," responded the director. "The church is already full, Mrs. Meritz."

"Ach, Gott in Himmel, mein lieber Gus," muttered Minnie to herself.

Right before the service began, the six pallbearers carried in the casket, which they placed on a stand at the front of the church. As the organist played the introduction to "Nearer My God to Thee," the service was underway. Following the reading of the Twenty-third Psalm, Pastor Brenner began his sermon. *"Gus,"* he said, *"had walked through the valley of the shadow of death, but he had feared no evil because God had been with him. Gus had been a man of faith."*

Yes, thought Lisetta, *a man of faith headed for heaven, but also very much a man who had enjoyed life on this earth. He had been so well liked by everyone.*

Following the sermon, the mourners lined up to view the body. This time, the family were the end of the long line. Lisetta watched as the funeral director slipped the gold wedding band from Gus's finger and handed it to Minnie before he closed the coffin for the last time.

Now began the long funeral procession to Prospect Hill Cemetery in Norfolk. Almost everyone at the funeral joined in the long trek to the cemetery. It was the same scenery that Lisetta had seen countless times on her way to Norfolk with her father – slightly rolling hills outside of Hoskins giving way to flatter ground as they processed along. *How beautifully green the meadows are*, she thought. She rolled down the window a little to see if she could catch the smell of the land. *Yes, there it was, that sweet clover smell.* A meadow lark was singing from its spot secluded in the grass, its song silvery and melodious.

Lisetta's eyes carried up to the top of the hill. A figure was standing there, watching the procession. *Or was it two figures?* She wondered. *Yes, a mother holding a child.* Lisetta did not know that the figure she saw was that of Nelia Getzmer, Paul's wife, holding her daughter Eileen. Nelia had wanted to come to the funeral, but she was due to deliver her second child at any time, and she was afraid to go far from home. However, she knew the time the procession would be moving along the road, and she wanted to be a part of it, even from this distance. As she stood and watched, it seemed to her that the procession would never end – like a long train moving slowly towards its destination. When the last vehicle in the procession had passed out of sight, she turned around and headed back to her house.

"That Gus Meritz sure had a lot of friends," she said to her little daughter, who didn't understand a word.

Chapter 9: Memories

The day after Gus's funeral, Lyle graduated from high school. Ed and Ella encouraged Minnie to attend the commencement exercises and to stop at their house for an early supper following the ceremony.

"Come in. Alles ist fertig," Ella said as she escorted them into the dining room.

"Is Aunt Lisetta coming?" asked young Lisetta.

"No. She's busy moving today."

"Moving!" exclaimed Minnie.

"Ja. She's rented a room on Third Street at the Krauses, not far from here."

Lyle perked up. (He had been dating Marcella Krause.)

"Poor Aunt Lisetta," said young Lisetta.

"I warned her that it would be too expensive to live in Norfolk on her farm income," said Minnie.

The subject of income was Ed's clue to enter the conversation.

"I don't mean to pry, Minnie, but did Gus leave you well enough off?"

"Ja." Minnie was proud of her financial situation. "Our land is debt free. We don't owe anything on the farm machinery or the livestock. The house is in good condition. Gus paid cash for the Buick. He took out a life insurance policy, which I can cash in if I need to, and he left fifteen thousand dollars in his savings account."

Ella was impressed but said nothing in response to this list of assets.

"You're a rich widow." said Ed.

"Ja. Gus was a good farmer. He knew how to manage, and he knew how to make money on cattle."

"If I were you, I'd stay away from investing in cattle right now. Everything's too high. Prices are sure to drop."

"Gus taught Lyle how to judge and care for cattle, and now that Lyle is through with school, he can help me manage the farm."

When supper was over, and Minnie, Lisetta and Lyle were leaving, Gus reminded Minnie that if she needed advice with the farm, he was ready to help.

"We'll be all right," said Lyle as he seated himself behind the wheel of the Buick. "Ma can depend on me to manage the farm."

"I hope she doesn't give him too much responsibility," Ed said to Ella after their guests were out of sight. "He's pretty wet behind the ears."

"Na, ja. He hasn't had to pinch pennies. I'll bet there weren't many young boys graduating today who got a new Chevrolet coupe."

*   *   *

During the summer, Lyle made good use of his new Chevy. He ran all of the business and social errands for Minnie, who stayed home on the farm and immersed herself in work. One Saturday afternoon, Lyle and Lisetta took a bucket of strawberries in to Aunt Ella's and visited a while. Then they stopped at the Krauses to deliver a basket of strawberries to their Aunt Lisetta. A petite, pretty young lady answered the door, invited them in, and introduced herself as Marcella to Lisetta and exchanged a smile with Lyle.

The following Saturday, Lyle suggested to his mother that Aunt Lisetta might like some fresh eggs. Minnie agreed, and Lyle was soon on his way to Norfolk with a basket of eggs. The next Saturday, Lyle suggested that he take in green beans and tomatoes from the garden.

"Lyle is sure being nice to your Aunt Lisetta these days. He must feel sorry for her," Minnie said to Lisetta.

"I think Lyle's in love."

"In love? With Aunt Lisetta?"

"No, Ma! With Marcella Krause."

"What's she like, this Marcella?"

"She's pretty and tiny."

"Doesn't sound right for a farmer. Anyway, Lyle is too young to fall in love."

"Is he? How old were you when you fell in love, Ma?"

"About Lyle's age, but your father was a few years older."

"How did you and Dad fall in love, Ma?"

"I don't know. It just happened. When we were growing up, we saw each other in church. Later we met at social gatherings, dances, mission festivals…."

"But when did you really notice him, or did he notice you as someone special?"

"It was one summer evening. Our family was going to a barn dance on the Muller farm. I remember that I had been working out in the field that day, helping with the oats harvest. My skin was tan, and my cheeks were flushed from working in the heat. My sister Ella had stayed inside, as she always did. 'You look like a peasant,' she said to me as we were driving to the dance. 'No man is going to want to dance with you tonight.'

'Shut up, you pale, skinny stick,' I said. 'I bet I get asked to dance more than you do.'"

"And did you, Ma?"

"Ja, I did. Ella sat on a stack of hay all evening, and I had four different partners in a row."

"Was one of them Dad?"

"No, not at first. I was hot and thirsty from dancing and was standing by the refreshment table, having a glass of lemonade, and your father came up to me and said, 'Minnie, you're looking sehr hubsch tonight.' I did look pretty, with my tan skin and my blue eyes. I was slim and muscular then. 'Danke schon, Gus,' I said. I remember looking up at him and thinking to myself what beautiful, warm eyes he had."

"And did he ask you to dance then, Ma?"

"No, we just stood there for a moment, looking at each other. Then he put his left hand on my waist and took my right hand in his and brought it up to his chest, and we started dancing."

"And did you dance the rest of the night with him?"

"Ja, I did. And Ella just sat there on that stack of hay. She was so jealous. On the way home, she said, 'That Gus Meritz sure looked like a peasant tonight.'

'Well,' I said, 'it looks like the peasants were the ones having all the fun tonight. Of course, if you're a lady, I suppose it is more fun to just sit around on a stack of hay.' She was as mad as a hornet at me and wouldn't speak to me for a week."

Lisetta laughed. "So, was that the night you fell in love?"

"Ja, I guess that was the night."

"Ma, do you think that you and Dad were destined to fall in love that night?"

"Ja. If I hadn't gone to that dance that night, maybe Gus and I wouldn't have fallen in love."

"So, do you think Aunt Lisetta was destined to end up alone?"

"I think she became an old maid because of her attitude. She was a farm girl; our parents were pioneers on the prairie. Lisetta should have been proud of our people, but she turned up her nose at farmers and their life."

"So, she never gave love a chance."

"Ja. Love is like a seed that's planted and has to sprout and grow."

"So, the dance that night was the seed sprouting for you and Dad?"

"Ja, I guess it was. We were ready to fall in love."

Minnie, who had been embroidering as she spoke, stopped her activity and sat quietly, a thoughtful look on her face.

Lisetta went up to her room and lay down on her bed. She remembered a Saturday evening when she was a young girl. She and Lyle were riding in the carriage with Minnie and Gus. As Gus drove into Hoskins, he headed for the Wetzlich Butcher Shop. He hitched the horse to a post, and they all got out and walked around to the side door of the shop. They climbed up a steep flight of narrow stairs and entered a room which extended the length of the shop. At one end stood a refreshment table, laden with cakes, cookies, lemonade, and coffee. At the opposite end was a stage. Three musicians were getting ready for the evening – a pianist, flutist, and violinist.

Lyle headed for a group of boys who were playing marbles. Lisetta sat down on a chair next to the dance floor. As the musicians played the opening bars to a schottische, Gus led Minnie to the floor. Lisetta watched as her parents gracefully bowed and glided and hopped together. Gus's eyes were on Minnie, who looked lovely in a long, flowered skirt and a white blouse with embroidery on the yoke. Her reddish-brown hair was pulled loosely back into a coil, several strands hanging free from the coil and wisping about her face.

When the music stopped, Gus and Minnie joined Lisetta. Then as the music started up again, Gus took Lisetta's hand and said, "I'm going to teach you how to dance tonight, young lady." And his rhythm was good and strong. He was easy to follow. And she was happy.....

Lisetta opened her eyes. She saw Gus's picture on her dresser. *That's all I have left*, she thought, *that picture and my memories.*

*   *   *

In the fall of 1928, Lisetta and Engie began their senior year at Norfolk High School. Lyle picked up Lisetta each Friday afternoon from Aunt Ella's and brought her back each Sunday afternoon. He was happy to do this because it gave him an opportunity to stop to see Marcella.

Lisetta was not eager to begin her senior year. She knew that she would have to do something other than studying when she graduated, but in her state of unhappiness, no line of work seemed desirable.

"Why don't you take some different types of classes, Zettie?" Aunt Ella suggested. "Maybe you can find out this year what interests you."

Lisetta took Aunt Ella's advice and signed up for Glee Club and a sewing class. She found that sewing temporarily lifted her spirits. There was a solace in running the sewing machine. As she pumped the wrought-iron treadle plate up and down with her feet and fed the material up to the needle with her hands, she forgot her discontentment. But when school was over for the day and she returned to Aunt Ella's, the unhappiness returned. The only thing she looked forward to was the weekend when she was back on the farm.

The young people in the neighborhood often got together on a Saturday evening for a party, taking turns playing host or hostess. Already this year, Lyle, Loretta, and Lisetta had been to the Liebs, the Lensers, and the Fenters for parties.

"Whose place are you going to tonight?" Minnie asked Lyle one Saturday evening in November.

"The Kiesters."

"Kiesters? I don't think I know them."

"Oliver and his mother moved onto the farm next to the Lingenbergs. They're originally from San Francisco. Oliver's father was a dentist there before they moved to Norfolk. I guess Dr. Kiester had relatives in this area. Anyway, he died not long after they moved to Norfolk, and Oliver was raised by his mother."

"Were they poor after his father died?" asked Lisetta.

"No, they owned some farms, including the one they just moved onto. Oliver comes home from Nebraska University on the weekends to be with his widowed mother."

At the Kiesters the young people at first listened to records, taking turns winding up the phonograph in the living room.

"Five foot two, eyes of blue, but oh what those five feet can do," sang Lyle, looking at Marcella. When Oliver put on "Yes, we have no bananas; we have no bananas today," Earl Muller jumped up and pretended to be a fruit vendor. As the evening wore on, Oliver set up card tables, and some of the party played pitch. Lisetta did not join in the game. She sat and visited with Rose Lenser, whom she hadn't seen for a while. Rose did her best to comfort her friend over the loss of her father, but Lisetta was there in body only, not in spirit.

*   *   *

One Saturday towards the end of April, Lisetta was especially gloomy.

"What's the matter?" Minnie asked.

"Everything, Ma. Everybody keeps asking me what I plan to do, and I still don't know. And now I have to write a poem for English class – we've been studying poetry as our final unit. It's due on Monday, and I don't know what to write about."

"Why don't you write about your father, Zettie? He would have liked that."

Lisetta went up to her room. For a while she stood at her window, which looked out to the lane. Then she propped herself up with pillows on her bed and wrote her poem. When she finished, she took it downstairs to read to Minnie.

Still in My Memory

I remember sitting on the porch, with

You in your rocker, I at your knee,

And I said, "Look at the pretty bird."

And you said, "That's a red-winged blackbird."

And its song was sweet in the sultry summer air,

And it still sounds sweet in my memory.

I remember looking down the lane for you,

Coming home in your smart roadster,

Waiting for the thick dust to settle,

Waiting for the harsh honk of your horn,

Waiting for you to wave when you saw me waiting,

And I'm waiting still in my memory.

I remember wearing my white dress, with

You nearby in your blue Sunday suit,

And you called our guests to attention,

And you lifted your wineglass to me

And said, "To my Liebchen, a young lady today,"

And that toast stays still in my memory.

And I remember that horrible hearse,

You in your box, I at the window,

And I said, "Listen to the owl hoot."

And you didn't hear; you couldn't hear.

And its hoot hung there in the heavy summer air,

And it hangs there still in my memory.

Minnie understood the first three verses but was puzzled with the fourth.

"The owl was already gone when your father was put into the hearse," she said.

"Ma, a poem doesn't have to be accurate. I was just describing how that owl still haunts me."

"Me, too," said Minnie.

(Actually, the author wrote this poem after her mother Lisetta told her the story of Gus's life and death.)

*   *   *

On May 23rd, Lisetta went to the high school for the last time. During the ceremony, she listened carefully to the commencement address. *Perhaps it will give me an idea about what to do,* she thought. *I'm tired of being undecided.* She looked over at Engie, who knew where she was headed. But Engie hadn't lost her father.

After commencement, the Meritzes walked to Ed and Ella's, where Ella had angel food cake, coffee, and lemonade ready. There were gifts for the two graduates. Engie and Lisetta each received a diamond ring from their parents. The two cousins compared their rings and then went upstairs to pack Lisetta's remaining belongings.

As Lisetta left that day, she had mixed feelings. She was proud to be a graduate, grateful for the ring, sad to leave her part-time home, and concerned about the future. She missed her father terribly. *When will this emptiness go away,* she wondered.

Part II Lisetta and Walter

Chapter 10: Plans

Shortly after graduation, Lisetta came down with strep throat, and Minnie called the new young Hoskins doctor to come out to the farm. When Doctor Brauer arrived, he took Lisetta's temperature, checked her over, gave her a shot, and handed Minnie a prescription to be filled at his drugstore in Hoskins.

"Who runs the drugstore when you're out on house calls?" asked Minnie.

"My wife. We live above the drugstore, and when I get a call, she comes down and takes over. "

"Convenient," said Minnie.

Doctor Brauer was anxious to learn about the Hoskins community. "What do you do for entertainment in Hoskins?" he asked Minnie.

"We have card parties, pinochle and pitch. Some of the men play poker at the pool hall or at the train depot. There's dancing in the summer at the Bruce Pavilion."

"Bruce? The Mayor of Hoskins?"

"Ja. He built the pavilion a few years back after the butcher shop closed."

"There was a butcher shop in Hoskins?"

"Ja. We used to dance above the Wetzlich Butcher Shop, owned by my husband's sister, Clara, and her husband."

"Why did the butcher chop close?"

"Not enough business. As more and more of the farmers got automobiles, they began driving into Norfolk to go to the larger shops. The Wetzlichs moved to California."

"And what do the young people do for entertainment?" he asked Lisetta.

"Same thing. Dance, play cards, parties."

"I'd like to get to know the community better. Perhaps we could work on something together this summer, like a play. The young people could perform it for the adults, perhaps at the Bruce Pavilion. Then we could have a reception afterwards – a community project. I could direct the rehearsals. Are you interested in the idea?"

"That would be good for Zettie," quickly responded Minnie. "She's been moping about since my husband Gus died a year ago." Lisetta nodded.

Two weeks later, Doctor Brauer had borrowed the scripts for "Under Twenty" from the drama teacher at Norfolk High School and had called for a meeting on the stage of the Bruce Pavilion. Sixteen young people attended the meeting, and Doctor Brauer passed out copies of the script to each of them.

"Read through the summary and the cast of characters," he said. "I want you to choose your own part. We'll also need a stage manager and some people in charge of props, tickets, makeup, and some prompters. If two people want the same part, we'll flip a coin. Have your part chosen by next Wednesday. We'll begin rehearsal at seven-thirty."

Lisetta went home and read the summary, in search of a part:

> In order to ease financial difficulties of the Farnum family,
>
> Peeks Farnum, after failing in an effort to suggest bankruptcy,
>
> plans a marriage for her sister Grace with a wealthy Westerner,
>
> Donald Brown. Diana Edgerton, however, shows a determination
>
> to get Don for herself, and Ted Rutherford turns up to woo Grace
>
> with a large inheritance. Meanwhile Peeks finds that she is in love
>
> with Don. In the end, the financial problems seem to untangle, as
>
> do the muddled love problems, and contentment settles over the
>
> Farnum household, especially over Peeks.

After the summary, Lisetta skimmed through the play, looking for the number of lines of the female characters. She decided that the character, Grace Farnum, would be right for her – not too many lines, not too few.

On Wednesday evening, after a few coin flips, the cast of characters was determined.

Ida Farnum, - Mother	*Helen Meritz*
Grace Farnum – Older Daughter	*Lisetta Meritz*
Peeks Farnum – Younger Daughter	*Rose Lenser*
Ronnie – Irish Maid	*Elsie Fenter*
Russell Farnum – Father	*Clarence Behmer*
Bill Boyd – House Detective	*Robbie Fenter*
Diana Edgerton – Young Business Woman	*Verona Buss*

Ted Rutherford – Young Would-Be Business Man   Walter Getzmer

Donald Brown – The Westerner   Earl Muller

"That's it," said Doctor Brauer. "Now let's begin by reading through Act I.

When Lisetta got home that evening from the rehearsal, her cheeks were flushed, and there was a sparkle in her eyes. Minnie was glad to see her looking happy for once.

*   *   *

On Saturday evening, Lyle announced that he was taking Marcella dancing at the Bruce Pavilion – Lawrence Welk and his band were scheduled.

"Take Zettie with you," said Minnie. "It would be good for her to get out of the house."

"Aw, Ma, she'll be a fifth wheel. Marcella and I want to be alone."

"Well, then, drive to Norfolk and get Marcella and then drive back here to pick up Zettie. After the dance, bring Zettie back here first. You'll still have enough time alone with your precious Marcella."

"O.K. You be ready to go as soon as I get back!" he ordered his sister.

Lisetta was ready when he returned. She was dressed in a blue-green voile dress, which hung gracefully on her slender figure. Her hair was waved and pulled loosely from her forehead, showing her widow's peak.

"I wish my hair were bobbed," she said to Minnie.

"Your hair is short enough. Those bobs make girls look like tramps. A young man wants a **nice** girl, Zettie."

Lisetta had been to the Bruce Pavilion for the play rehearsals, but this was her first dance since her father's death. When the three entered the pavilion, they joined the Mullers at a table on the left side of the dance floor. As Lisetta looked around, she saw some of her friends from the play, but most of the people were strangers to her. Lawrence Welk's band was popular, and people had come from Norfolk, Winside, Hadar, and Stanton to dance.

The band was playing a polka. The wind, string, and percussion players were on the stage, and Lawrence Welk was in the center of the dance floor, playing his accordion while he moved around in a circle. The couples on the dance floor polkaed around him. One of the couples, Lisetta noticed, was Walter Getzmer and a young lady she didn't recognize.

"Come on and dance with me," said Earl Muller, taking Lisetta by the hand as the band began playing "Doggie in the Window." When they returned to their table after the dance,

Lisetta looked across the room and saw that Walter was seated with his brother Ferd and Ferd's date. As Lisetta watched, a girl in a short-fringed dress approached Walter. The girl stood there twisting her long beads while leaning her bobbed head towards Walter. Then she pulled him up, and they headed for the dance floor. As they danced to the "Blue Skirt Waltz," Lisetta noticed that the girl kicked off her shoes and pressed herself against Walter. A pang of jealousy hit Lisetta. Throughout her father's long illness and her bereavement, she had not thought much about Walter, but now, seeing him here, the old feelings surfaced.

"Who is that dancing with Walter?" she asked Earl.

"That's a girl from Winside. She's not your type, Zettie, and neither is Walter. I'm your type. Let's dance!" But he was too late. Lisetta had already nodded yes to Robbie Fenter, who had approached the table behind Earl's back.

Throughout the evening, Lisetta danced with each of the boys in the play, except for Walter, and with two young strangers. She was happy that she had not been a wallflower. When Earl reached out his hand to her as the band played "Save the Last Dance for Me," she was sorry to see the evening end.

On the following Wednesday at play rehearsal, Walter said to her, "I saw you at the dance on Saturday night. You danced a lot with Earl. Are you sweet on him, Lisetta?"

"No." She blushed and changed the topic. "Are you enjoying being the Young Would-Be Business Man?"

"Yes, Grace, how does it feel to be the Older Daughter?"

"Ancient. Oh, oh, we're up next."

Lisetta knew her part well. As she said her lines, she could tell that Walter thought that she was smart. Perhaps even a little pretty? And as she listened to his lines, she liked his warm tenor voice and the way he carried himself. *He still has those straight, high shoulders,* she thought

At each rehearsal, the Young Would-Be Business Man and the Older Daughter found time to visit with each other. During the dress rehearsal, they were standing together behind the curtain, waiting for the next scene.

"Are you enjoying your job at the bank?" Lisetta asked.

"Very much. Mr. Rohrke is great to work for. And he's sold his insurance business to me as a sideline."

"How did you get the job in the bank, Walt?"

"Mr. Rohrke asked Pastor Brenner to recommend a young man for the job, and Pastor recommended me."

"Lucky you! You're not just a Would-Be Business Man, are you, Walt?"

"No. My future looks pretty golden. Business is flourishing at the bank. I should do well. How about you, Lisetta? Any plans for the future?"

"Ja, I've finally decided to apply to Wayne Normal. This fall I'll start studying to be a teacher."

"You'll be a good one, Lisetta. You were always so intent on doing well in school." He smiled. "I remember that first day at country school when you were upset because you couldn't read the assignments on the board."

"I know. You helped me, and I thought you were so nice."

"Will you be staying at Wayne next year?"

"Only during the week. On the weekends I'll come back home."

"Good. Then I'll still see you from time to time."

Lisetta smiled at Walter, who was looking directly into her eyes. His eyes shifted to her lips. Leaning down, he kissed her quickly and firmly. "Next scene!" Doctor Brauer's voice sounded through the curtain.

On the evening of the play, there was no opportunity for Lisetta and Walter to have another extended conversation, but they smiled at each other throughout the evening, and there was a noticeable spark in their scenes together.

"Walt Getzmer has grown up, hasn't he?" Minnie remarked on the way home.

"Ja, Ma. He's working in the bank now. He thinks he'll do well in business."

"Huh! A clerk in a bank! Not much future in that."

*   *   *

A week later, Minnie and Lyle helped load Lisetta's belongings into the Buick and headed for the women's dormitory at Wayne. The countryside was festooned with the brilliant yellow flowers of the goldenrod plants, which had sprung up in pastures and along roads and fences. Some of the erect plants were eight feet high, with sessile leaves and flower clusters on slightly-branched stems.

"Look how beautiful the goldenrod are, Ma!" Lisetta remarked.

"Ja, and so many of them. That shows what a good summer we've had. The hay has been plentiful this season. The oats crop was big, and I think the corn will be, too. Farming is a good life, Zettie. Don't forget it."

"Ja," said Lyle. "The markets are all up, the hog market, the cattle market. And corn is selling for eighty cents a bushel. When I sell our corn and cattle this fall, I'll have enough to repay those notes and then some."

"What notes?" asked Lisetta.

"A business deal between Lyle and me," said Minnie. "Nothing for you to be concerned about."

Lisetta was not concerned. Her future looked bright. She had a plan and a dream. She sat back and watched the brilliant goldenrod whizzing by.

When Minnie, Lyle, and Lisetta arrived at Wayne Normal, they drove to Neihardt Hall, named after the Nebraska author, John G. Neihardt. There they were greeted by the housekeeper, Mother Harmon. She recited the house rules to Lisetta: no smoking or drinking alcoholic beverages in the dormitory; no music after nine o'clock; curfew at nine on weekdays and eleven on weekends; male visitors allowed only in the living room.

Minnie liked these rules.

"You won't have any problems with Lisetta," she said to Mrs. Harmon. "She knows how to behave."

Later that evening, after Minnie and Lyle had left, Laura Harmon, Mother Harmon's daughter introduced herself and showed Lisetta around the campus. As they walked around, she pointed out the various instruction halls, the cafeteria, the men's dormitory, the gymnasium, and the library. Before going back to Neihardt Hall, Laura took Lisetta to the Willow Bowl, an island of lush green grass forming the center of the bowl, surrounded by beautiful willow trees with long, green, lacy branches. Laura explained that the Bowl was the spot where graduation exercises were held, but that she and her boyfriend Red used it as a meeting spot between classes. She confided that they had secretly become engaged.

"Do you have a beau?" she asked Lisetta.

"There's someone I like very much. This summer we were in a play, and he kissed me behind the stage."

"Ah ha! Sounds like the beginning of a romance."

When they returned to the hall, Engie had moved in. Lisetta introduced her cousin, and Laura explained to them both about the noontime dances, the black bottom and the jitterbug, which the girls danced to the accompaniment of a resident jazz pianist.

By the end of the week, Lisetta and Engie were quite good at the new dances and were happy with their classes and college in general. But as they traveled along towards Hoskins and Norfolk, they did not realize that their futures were precarious.

The date was September 7th, 1929, the day that the stock market took its first big plunge. Throughout the spring and summer months of Herbert Hoover's first days in the White House, the stock market had climbed higher and higher, continuing the golden prosperity of the previous years. During this time, speculation had gotten out of hand as more and more Americans had developed a mania for easy wealth. Widows had speculated with their pension money; businessmen had taken out loans on their businesses; farmers had mortgaged their land for improvements; gamblers had bought stocks on margin; banks had made unsecured promissory notes.

The Hoskins farmers had been spoiled by the prosperity of the twenties. They had forgotten the hard times, the times of drought and financial depression. Some of them had taken loans on their land to purchase machinery or to buy more land. Some, like Minnie and Lyle, had invested heavily in livestock.

At first, the September 7th stock market plunge did not worry the Hoskins farmers unduly. But when it continued to fall, along with prices of farm products, they became alarmed by the nation-wide panic that began on Thursday, October 24th. Thirteen million shares of stock changed hands on that day. Some heavy speculators, morose over the loss of their fortunes, jumped out of buildings or off bridges.

On October 28th and 29th, more than thirteen million shares changed hands. As prices continued to drop steadily, the stock market began to affect more than the stock speculators. Foreign trade fell sharply. Factories closed. One in every four city workers lost his job. Banks closed. The buying power of the nation was paralyzed. Farmers, unable to sell their commodities, lost their income. One-fourth of the American farmers lost their farms as mortgages were foreclosed.

Minnie and Lyle had been too optimistic. Minnie had loaned her entire savings, fifteen thousand dollars, to Lyle for livestock purchases. When farm commodities dropped, Lyle took a hefty loss on the sale of the cattle. Nor could they afford to sell any grain at the current prices. Minnie's working capital was gone.

Minnie remembered that Ed had offered to help her shortly after Gus's death. She got out the Buick and drove alone to Norfolk to see Ed.

> "I warned you that prices were sure to drop, Minnie, and not to invest in cattle. And you gave too much responsibility to Lyle. He was too young to handle it."

> "I know." She reached into her purse. "I have these notes that Lyle has signed, but I don't know how he can repay the money. The problem is, we don't have any cash to operate with. Do you think I could get a loan from the bank?"

"Well, you can't get an unsecured loan, and I don't think you can take out a loan against your land right now, Minnie. Besides, most of the banks around here are closed."

"What can I do, Ed?"

"Well, Minnie, it looks like you're just going to have to eat those notes. Lyle can't repay you, that's for sure. I wish we could help you, but I couldn't sell my grain this fall either. We all have to just pull in our belts."

Minnie straightened her back in determination. "Unless there's a drought, we won't starve," she said. "My granaries are full of grain, enough to feed the livestock we have left for some time. We can live off that and my garden. Lisetta will have to get a job as soon as she can, and the taxes will just have to wait until next year."

When Minnie got back to the farm, she called Lisetta down to the parlor for a talk. As her mother explained the situation regarding the notes and the working capital, Lisetta quietly listened, wondering what was coming next.

"I know you like college, Zettie, and you have been thinking of going for four years, but I don't have any more money. This year is paid for already, but there's no money for next year. You need to get a job as soon as possible, Zettie!"

Lisetta knew that fifteen thousand dollars was a very large sum of money. She wondered how anyone could have gone through that amount since her father's death. But, she had been taught not to question Minnie, and so she said nothing.

When Minnie finished, Lisetta went up to her room. She had a date with Walter in the evening, and she wanted to look her best. As she dressed, she thought about the future. Teaching in high school was out of the question now. It would have to be country school. She could get her credential by the end of the summer and begin teaching in the fall if a rural position opened up, but she wondered about Walter's future. The Hoskins Bank was sure to close.

Walter called for Lisetta after supper, and they drove to Norfolk in his green Chevie coupe. After seeing "Broadway Melody" at the theater, they went to Tranos' Ice Cream Parlor, where they seated themselves in a booth.

"What are your plans, Walt, if the Hoskins Bank closes?" Lisetta asked as she sipped her phosphate.

"It will close. The federal government is putting pressure on the bank. I've thought of going to Norfolk Business College." He smiled, "I guess that really would make me a Would-Be Businessman."

"Could you afford that, Walt?"

"I could afford to go for six months. I've saved some money at the bank, and I have a little income from the insurance business."

"I suppose you'll study accounting and bookkeeping."

"Ja, and business law and real estate and typing. Maybe the business courses would help me get another job. What about you, Lisetta? Still planning to be a teacher?"

"Planning is the wrong word. My mother is in charge of my future. She has lost a lot of money, and I have to get a job as soon as possible – in country school, if I can."

"You'd like teaching." He smiled at her. "And your students would like you, especially the boys. I can see them now when pretty Miss Meritz comes into the schoolhouse."

Lisetta blushed. "I'll be eighteen soon. In their eyes, I'll be an old maid."

Walter smiled. "Come on, old maid. I'll take you home."

As they drove towards Hoskins, Walter was humming a tune from the movie they had just seen. Lisetta remembered the words:

> *"You were meant for me.*
>
> *I was meant for you.*
>
> *Nature patterned you and when she was done,*
>
> *You were all the good things rolled into one."*

Lisetta loved his soft tenor voice. *The good things rolled into one – that's you, Walter*, she thought.

Chapter 11: Mrs. Meritz, Mrs. Meritz, and Miss Meritz

In the spring of 1930, Lyle announced to Minnie and Lisetta that he and Marcella were engaged and planned to be married on August 31st, the day of Lisetta's 18th birthday. Marcella wanted Lisetta to be her maid of honor, and Lisetta felt honored. The couple planned to honeymoon in Yellowstone Park and then return to the farm to live.

As spring progressed, Minnie visualized a house with one man and three grown women and decided that that would be far from ideal. Perhaps, she thought, this would be the time to claim the seven thousand dollars from Gus's life insurance policy.

"Zettie," she said on a Saturday morning, "we're going to Norfolk to purchase a lot."

"A lot of what?"

"A lot to build a house on, for us to live in, so Lyle and Marcella can live here."

"I didn't think you had any money, Ma."

Minnie explained that she had not wanted to use Gus's life insurance money as income or as working capital. But with a real estate investment, she would be saving the money rather than spending. As Minnie was talking, Lisetta was wondering how her mother would be able to adjust to city life, but she kept silent, seeing how determined Minnie was.

In no time, Minnie's determination led to action. The lot she purchased was next door to the Wells residence on Nebraska Avenue. Dr. Wells was a well-known dentist in Norfolk. Across the street lived an attorney and his wife. Minnie would have dependable, well-to-do neighbors.

"You might meet a young Norfolk businessman," Minnie said to Lisetta. Lisetta did not answer. She had already met a young Hoskins "would-be businessman."

Following the purchase of the lot, Minnie visited the Miller brothers, who had built the Meritz home on the farm when Lisetta was a little girl. Minnie described to them what she wanted, and they promised to have the house ready for Minnie after the second week in September, when Lyle and Marcella would be returning from their honeymoon.

Early in the summer, Lisetta went to a dance at the Bruce Pavilion. Earl Muller, who was there, mentioned that his sister would be in the sixth grade this year and was wondering who her teacher would be. The next day, Lisetta contacted Ernest Puls, the Chairman of District 85 School Board.

"Well, Lisetta," he said when the interview was over, "I'm happy we'll have a teacher who lives right here in the neighborhood." He handed her a key to the building. "I guess when I see you next, I'll have to call you Miss Meritz." Lisetta was thinking to herself that she would have to ask Lyle and Marcella to take her in as a boarder so that she could stay in the area.

All summer, Lisetta prepared for her teaching job. She would have eighteen students ranging in grades from one through eight. She read through the course of study for each grade level, as outlined by the State of Nebraska. Then she made a broad yearly plan for each class, determining how much material to cover each week. Finally, she planned in detail the lessons for the first week of school.

Towards the end of the summer, she went to the school to get the building physically ready for the school year. It was situated at the corner of two crossroads, with a corner porch looking southeast from the square building. The porch was full of leaves and dirt that had blown onto it during the summer. Lisetta unlocked the door, went into the basement, where the janitorial supplies were kept, and brought up a broom, a dustpan, a bucket of sweeping compound, and some rags. First, she swept off the porch. Then she tackled the inside. She moved all of the desks to one side of the classroom, spread sweeping compound over the floor, and swept the area. Then she pushed the desks to the other side, swept the compound over the floor on that side, and then into the cloakrooms and the book depository. When she had finished sweeping, she scooped the compound into the bucket and carried it back into the basement. She would use this same compound again and again in the coming days until it was no longer effective.

Her next task was deciding where to place the different grades. She arranged the desks in sections and then carried the books from the depository to the desks, sliding them onto the shelves under the desktops. She dusted the tops of the desks and then gathered pencils, pens, inkwells, and erasers from the depository and placed one of each on each desktop. Next, she wiped down all of the blackboards with a damp rag, gathered up all of the erasers, carried them outside, and pounded them clean. Finally, she organized the teacher's supplies in the desk on the platform.

Lisetta was glad that the school board had already done the outdoor work in preparation for the school year. They had mowed the prairie grass on the school lot, had poured chemicals down the outhouse toilets, patched the shingle roof, washed the windows, and had hauled coal and wood to the schoolhouse and scooped it down the chute into the basement. She knew that it would be her job to get to the school early on winter mornings, to load the furnace, start the fire, and have the building warm by the time her pupils arrived. But the coal and the wood were there, waiting for the winter weather to come.

*   *   *

On August 31ˢᵗ, Lyle and Marcella were married at St. Paul's Lutheran Church, Marcella's home church, and the home church of the early pioneers. Minnie had been here many times throughout the years, first with her parents, later with Gus. Since pioneer days, the original building had been replaced by a larger, more beautiful structure. As she sat in the front pew, waiting for the ceremony to begin, she reflected on her life with Gus.

By the time the honeymooners returned from Yellowstone, Lisetta had already begun her first year of teaching, still living in her old bedroom on the farm and walking to and from school through the pastures each morning and late afternoon. On her first morning as a teacher, she had picked a handful of white prairie asters and deep-blue, funnel-shaped gentians. The clusters of gentian flowers were still closed in early morning, but she knew they would be beautiful when they opened in mid-morning. Entering the classroom, she had just enough time to put the flowers in a vase on her desk before her pupils began to arrive. Some of them were boys and girls she already knew as neighbors; some were relatives of classmates she had had in school; the remaining ten she recognized, but she needed to learn their names.

As her students greeted each other, Lisetta reflected on her own first day in country school when Miss Martin had assigned each student a seat and had recited the rules to follow. During the summer, Lisetta had been thinking about discipline for her class, and she had decided that her pupils could choose their own seats within their class section. She would establish rules as the need arose rather than to anticipate naughty behavior.

Lisetta's goals for the year were to have her students like and respect her and to achieve through hard work. By the end of the first week of school, Lisetta knew that she was liked. She was invited by her pupils to come outside at recess time to play softball with them. Later in the year, when the snow prevented a softball game, she was invited to play Fox and Goose. If the weather prevented them from going outside to play, she often participated inside in a game of Button, Button, Who's Got the Button.

As for naughty behavior, occasionally she had to keep one of the boys after school. But that meant that he had to walk home alone instead of enjoying the companionship of his classmates, and a second dose of detention was usually not needed.

Lisetta did not expect her students to work any harder than she was prepared to work herself. Her school day began at seven-thirty in the morning when she left the house to walk to school. When she got there, she loaded the furnace and started the fire. Then she went upstairs to write assignments on the blackboard. When classes were over for the day, she stayed to help students or to work on lessons for the next day. Then she cleaned the blackboards and swept the floor. Sometimes Walter came by from his day at Norfolk Business College and picked her up as she was walking home.

When she got home, she helped Marcella prepare supper and clean up afterwards. Then she went up to her room to work on the "stumpy" arithmetic problems she had assigned her eighth graders. The answers were in the teacher's edition of the *Milne Arithmetic Book*, but not the solutions, and she wanted to be ready to demonstrate the solutions to her class the next day. At ten o'clock she turned out her light and fell asleep with arithmetic problems swimming in her head.

Lisetta enjoyed her school work as well as the social activities which accompanied it. For her and for her students, as well, the highlight of the school year was the Christmas program, put on for family and friends shortly before Christmas vacation. Lisetta taught the entire class Christmas carols to sing, and each grade planned a skit for the occasion. The program was combined with a box social. Boxes were auctioned off to the highest bidder, with the money going into the school fund. In preparation for the event, Lisetta decorated an old hat box with red crepe paper and trimmed the top with white paper roses, which she tacked to a green satin ribbon. Inside the box, she put fried chicken, home-baked bread, pumpkin pie, and apples.

The evening began with the program. Several of the older boys had strung up curtains at the front of the teacher's platform, creating a stage. All of the students crowded onto the make-shift stage to sing carols for the first quarter of an hour. Then, as the pupils joined their parents in the audience, the curtains were pulled.

When they opened, Helen Muller and Herbert Wantoch, two of Lisetta's youngest pupils, stood on the stage. Herbert had his right hand in his pocket.

"I'll bet you can't guess what I have in my pocket," he said to Helen.

Helen first guessed candy, then a pencil, an eraser, finally a penny.

"Give up? A hole!"

As the audience, laughed, Helen and Herbert stepped down to make way for the next skit.

Following the program, the box social began, with Lisetta's box being the first to be auctioned off. No one was supposed to know whose it was, but Walter had found out and managed to outbid the other contenders.

"You're looking as pretty as your box tonight, Miss Meritz," he said as they sat down at a desk to eat their supper. Lisetta blushed.

"Do you remember when I sat behind you and dipped your pigtail in my inkwell?"

"Yes, I do, Walter Getzmer! You wouldn't get away with that in my classroom."

"Oh, I don't know, Miss Meritz. I heard that you're not so strict. You even play softball with your class."

"Yes, I do."

"I understand that one recess you were up to bat. You hit the ball into the outfield and ran lickity split around the bases, trying for a home run. The last few yards you started sliding into the base, but just before you reached it, you were tagged out. *'Dammit!'* you said and stamped your foot."

"Ja," Lisetta agreed. "I should have made that home run!"

*   *   *

In May of 1931 after school was out, Lisetta moved into 1208 Nebraska Avenue with Minnie. During her year of teaching, she had saved enough out of her $50 a month salary for tuition at Norfolk Junior College. Her year of teaching had given her a new appreciation for learning, and she was anxious to work towards a degree.

Minnie was happier now that Lisetta was back home, but she still missed the farm. During the day, she frequently drove to Hoskins to visit the farms, to check the livestock, and to keep an eye on the pastures, the oats, and the cornfields. At night she dreamed about the alfalfa rolling in waves across the land on a windy day, or about walking down a row of tall corn, brushing her shoulders against the long, arching leaves; sometimes about the cottonwood trees standing tall, their shiny leaves glinting in the sunlight; or the whir of the windmill, its sails going round and round to fill the water tank with cool well water; and then reaching her hand down the side of the tank to feel the spongy green moss. Gus was seldom in her dreams anymore, but her love of the land remained.

In Norfolk, Minnie tried to carry the farm into the city by planting a large vegetable garden in the backyard. Now that Lisetta was home again, Minnie expected her to help with the canning of the ripe vegetables and fruits. During the week, Lisetta attended classes, but on Saturday, Minnie needed her to help her in the kitchen. It was Lisetta's job to peel, dice, or cut the items for the jars while Minnie prepared the sauce, put the items into jars, and secured the lids. Then Lisetta carried them into the basement where Minnie had put up shelves in a cool room she called "the fruit cellar."

Lisetta was happy when evening came and she could escape from the kitchen. Not only was the drudgery finished for the day, but she was expecting to see Walter. Throughout the summer, they had been dating steadily, sometimes driving to Hoskins for a dance at the Bruce Pavilion, sometimes going out for an evening drive. Lisetta enjoyed most the times they went for drives in the countryside. They usually had a destination: to visit Walter's parents in Hoskins or Ferd and his wife Alverna or Emil and Paul.

This particular evening, Walter and Lisetta headed for Emil's. As they left the lights of Norfolk behind them, a harvest moon was just peeking over the eastern horizon. The yellow moon was so large, it seemed to be hogging the sky, pushing the tiny, white stars out of its path.

"Look how big the moon is!" exclaimed Lisetta.

"Shine on, shine on harvest moon up in the sky. I ain't had no lovin' since January, February, June, and July," sang Walter in his soft tenor voice.

He reached across and put his arm around Lisetta's shoulders, and she snuggled up against him as they drove towards Emil's farm. When they reached the farm, they parked in front of the barn and started up the hill towards the house.

"To think that this old house was once my home, and then your home," Lisetta said.

88

"Ja, and now it's Emil's home."

"Is he renting it from your parents?"

"No, he owns this farm now. That's how my folks could afford to retire to the acreage on the edge of Hoskins. By the way, don't be surprised if a lot of my relatives are here tonight."

"Is it a party?"

"No, but Ferd and Alverna and their little boy Ralph live on the farm right over there to the west of Emil's, and they might be visiting, too. And Paul lives here now with his two little girls."

"Ma and I went to Nelia's funeral. Little Eileen and Elaine didn't know what it was all about, poor things."

When they entered the house, the little girls, still missing their mother, clamored around Lisetta, pulling her skirts for attention. Lisetta and Walter divided their attention between the little ones and the adults until Paul took the girls up to bed and Ferd and Alverna took Ralph home. Then they settled into an adult visit.

"I had a visitation again this last week," said Emil.

"Oh?" responded Walter.

"Ja. About three o'clock in the morning. I woke up and saw a little girl standing at the foot of my bed. She had on a white dress. Her blond hair was in curls, and she had daisies in her hair. She didn't speak, just stood there looking at me. And suddenly she was gone."

"You know what Mother always said about visitations," said Paul.

"What was that?" asked Lisetta.

"That someone had died," answered Walter. "She got a letter from Germany telling her about it, both times."

"Has someone in the neighborhood died?" Lisetta addressed Emil.

"Not this neighborhood. But a little girl in Winside fell off her horse and broke her neck."

"Did you have a visitation, Emil, before Nelia died?" Paul asked.

"No, Paul. But Nelia didn't die a sudden death." Paul nodded.

"Ferd and I had a visitation once about ten years ago," said Walter.

"Where?" asked Lisetta.

"Right here, in this old house."

"I think this old house is haunted," said Paul.

"Well, it was that night. The whole family had gone to bed, and Ferd and I were asleep. We both woke up when we heard someone knocking. Three times. Knock, knock, knock!" Walter rapped the table with his knuckles. 'Is that you, Ma?' I yelled. "There was no answer. Then we heard someone starting up the stairs, slowly, step by step. The footsteps didn't sound normal. Ferd was so scared, he hid under the covers. I was scared, too, but for some reason, I couldn't take my eyes off the door. Then I saw a light and a faint figure come through the door, walk by the bed, and pass out of the room."

"Ooh!" exclaimed Lisetta. "Did someone die?"

"Ja, but we didn't know who. The next morning, we talked about it at breakfast, and Mother said, 'Just vait, boys, someone you know died.' And when we got to town the next day, we found out that our best friend, Richard, had died."

"I remember that," said Lisetta. "My parents talked about it. Richard had gotten ahold of some strong illegal hooch and died of alcohol poisoning. Ma took the opportunity to caution Lyle and me against strong drink."

"Would you like a glass of homemade wine before you go?" asked Emil with a twinkle in his eye. Walter smiled and shook his head.

On the way back to Norfolk, the moon was directly overhead. It had changed from a golden yellow to a brilliant white, casting an unearthly spell over the land.

"Paul talked about Nelia tonight," Lisetta said. "I can still remember her standing at the top of that hill when Dad's funeral procession passed by. I didn't know until later who she was."

"Ja," said Walter. "She died not long after that, after Elaine was born."

"I heard that she lost her mind."

"Ja. The doctor diagnosed her illness as St. Louis encephalitis."

"What is that?"

"Swelling of the brain. They think the disease comes from a mosquito bite. The mosquito bites an infected horse or a pigeon or a prairie chicken, and then bites a human. I know they had horses on that farm, and of course, pigeons always hang around barns."

"Emil said she didn't die suddenly."

"No, she didn't. At first, she became sleepy and lost energy. Then her personality changed. She'd always been sweet and jolly and easygoing. Suddenly she became violent and started talking in filthy language. Paul was afraid she might harm Eileen and Elaine; so, he put her in the Verges Sanitarium in Norfolk, and she died shortly after."

"Poor soul," said Lisetta. "You know, Paul was a pallbearer when Dad died."

"I know." Walter put his arm around Lisetta and gave her a squeeze.

*   *   *

In the fall of the year, when Lisetta was well into her year at Norfolk Junior College, her friend Laura called from Wayne.

"Mother and I would like to visit you this weekend," she said. "May we come?"

"Of course! I have so much to tell you."

"And I have a lot to tell you, Zettie."

Minnie and Lisetta picked them up at the train depot on Saturday morning and drove them to 1208 Nebraska Avenue.

"A lovely house," said Mrs. Harmon as they approached the porch. Minnie liked to be complimented, and she enjoyed Mrs. Harmon's company. The two mothers had much in common: both were middle-aged widows; both had daughters in college; both were struggling with the financial difficulties of the depression.

After lunch, Lisetta and Laura left their mothers to visit and went outside for a walk. It was a beautiful autumn day. Nebraska Avenue was lined with Chinese elm trees on both sides. The trees formed an arbor over the avenue, their branches meeting high overhead. The leaves had turned yellow but had not yet begun dropping to the ground. As Lisetta and Laura crossed the avenue, they were aware of the yellow canopy overhead, providing a protective covering to their conversation. Their voices, as they talked, were soft and secretive.

"I have something to tell you, Zettie."

"And I have something to tell you. But you first."

"It's a secret. Mother knows about it, but no one else."

She stopped and looked directly at Lisetta.

"Red and I are married."

"Married!"

"Yes. We drove to Elk Point, South Dakota over Labor Day and got married there."

"Congratulations, Laura! But why are you keeping it a secret?"

91

"We can't afford to live together. My expenses at Wayne Normal are free while Mother is at Neihardt Hall, but they wouldn't be if the school knew I was married."

"I see."

"Red and I are together most of the time, but we don't really live together."

"Laura, why didn't you just wait until you both graduate?"

"Zettie, we were too much in love. We wanted to belong to each other."

"Oh, Laura! How romantic!"

"Now you, Zettie. What's your secret?"

"I'm in love with Walt Getzmer, and I think he's in love with me, too. We've been together all summer. Everybody thinks of us as Walt and Zettie. The problem is, he doesn't have a steady job. Right now, he's picking corn on his brother Emil's farm."

"Didn't he used to work at the bank in Hoskins?"

"Ja, but that closed after the crash. You know what it's like. Unless you're a teacher these days, it's almost impossible to get a steady job."

"Do you think he'll ask you to marry him?"

"I don't know, but even if he did, I'm not sure we could get married right now."

"Zettie, if your love is strong enough, you'll find a way."

You'll find a way. When the visit with Laura ended, her words kept ringing in Lisetta's ears, like church bells.

Chapter 12: The Secret

By mid-November, all of the corn had been picked, and there was no more work in the fields. With corn at thirty-two cents a bushel, most of the farmers did not bother to sell it. Why lose money? They simply stored the corn in their corncribs, to be used for livestock feed.

When Walter came to call on Lisetta on a Saturday evening, he had just picked the last of the corn at Emil's, having earned very little since Emil did not plan to sell his corn. But Walter still had several hundred dollars in savings from his salary at the bank. Enough, he thought, for a while yet.

The destination this evening was the Bruce Pavilion, where they would meet Laura and Red. As they left the house, it was already dark. Minnie turned on the porch light so that they could see their way to the car. The air was crisp and cold. Lisetta, wearing a woolen coat, a cloche hat, and mittens, felt her breath coming out in a vapor as she spoke.

"I think it will snow tonight."

"Ja," said Walter. "But there's no wind. I don't think we'll need chains."

The land was desolate and bare as they drove towards Hoskins. All of the lush green of the summer and the bright yellows and reds of the autumn were gone, and the ground was not yet covered with its protective, white winter blanket. It seemed to be in limbo, between life and death. Lisetta shivered and snuggled up close to Walter.

"Walt," she said, "would you like to join my family for Thanksgiving dinner?"

"Yes, Lisetta, I would like to, but I can't. I'll be in Sholes at Thanksgiving time."

"Sholes?"

"Ja. Sholes, Nebraska – you know that little town north of here. My brother Dick has a grocery store there, and he needs my help."

"I don't understand."

"Well, Dick's wife Minnie got depressed and ran away, and Dick is going to Chicago to `try to find her. He asked me to take care of the store while he's gone, and I'm driving to Sholes tomorrow."

"When will you be back, Walt?"

"When Dick finds Minnie, I suppose. I don't really know."

Walter was silent, and Lisetta responded by more silence. *He doesn't know*, she thought, *and he doesn't seem to care*. They drove the rest of the way in silence. When they got to the pavilion, Laura and Red were already there. Ordinarily, Lisetta would have been happy to see her friend in such a state of bliss, but tonight it only intensified her own unhappiness. And then, to make matters worse, Adeline, the flapper from Winside, was there. She pulled Walter to the dance floor, leaving Lisetta sitting alone. Lisetta went to the ladies' room with Laura. When she returned to the table, the band had just started playing the final number. Walter was waiting for her. He took her hand and led her to the dance floor. The vocalist began singing: "Goodnight sweetheart, 'til we meet tomorrow." Lisetta's eyes welled with tears. Walter was going away, perhaps for good. She wanted to tell him not to go, but Dick needed him, and it was not her place to enter into his family matters.

*   *   *

By Christmastime, Lisetta had not heard from Walter.

"Walt must still be in Sholes," she said to Minnie. "Maybe I should send him a letter

for Christmas."

"Has he written to you, Zettie?"

"No, Ma."

"Nice girls don't run after boys. If he really cared for you, he would write to you. Forget him, Zettie. He's not the only rooster in the barnyard."

Lisetta tried to forget Walter. She went dancing at Madison with her Uncle Harry's younger brother. He was a smooth dancer and a sharp dresser, but she did not care for him. She went with Earl Muller to the movies, but Earl had never become more than a friend to her. She and a friend from Wayne Normal double-dated with Laura and Red, but he was no substitute for Walter.

One evening in March, when Lisetta was at the Bruce Pavilion with Earl, she saw Walter with Adeline. *So, he's back*, she thought, *and he didn't even bother to contact me*. Lisetta did her best throughout the evening, pretending she was having a good time, but when the evening was over, she cried.

"I'm tired of seeing you mope around," Minnie said to Lisetta one day towards the end of March. "You should have my problems."

"What problems, Ma?"

"Money problems."

"Again? What about the seven thousand dollars, the life insurance money?"

"All gone. Building this house. Living expenses."

"But you get farm rent from Lyle, don't you?"

"Only for the oats and the corn. I don't charge him pasture rent, and no one made much from oats and corn this year. I don't know what I'm going to do, Zettie, but I need to do something soon."

Minnie had always been a woman of action. A week later, she took the first steps in a new survival plan. She rented 1208 Nebraska Avenue to Milo Hansen, who had retired when the Hoskins depot closed. Minnie planned to use the rent money for operating expenses on her farm. She would move across the road from Lyle onto the land that Hank had farmed before he moved to Chicago. The house on that land had become uninhabitable, but it was a good enough place to temporarily store her furniture.

Minnie planned to build a house on the land, hopefully her third and final piece of construction. Mrs. Koerbur, a friend in Norfolk, had agreed to loan her the money, and Charlie Ohlund, a carpenter from Hoskins, had quoted her a good price for the construction. Charlie promised to have the house built within five months and the basement ready by the end of May. Minnie planned to live in the rooms in the basement until the upstairs was finished. She had worked out where she would stay and how she would support herself during the next few months. Laura Bech, her brother Gus's wife, had not been well for some time. Minnie visited Gus and Laura and offered her services as a cook and housekeeper in exchange for room and board, and Gus and Laura accepted the offer. Finally, Minnie visited Ed and Ella, who agreed to have Lisetta with them until the end of the school year.

"Don't worry about me, Ma," Lisetta said when Minnie told her about her plan. "I'll be fine at Aunt Ella's. But what about you? A cook and housekeeper at Uncle Gus's? You know how you hate his crude language and his dirty jokes."

"I can take care of your Uncle Gus. I'll put him in his place. Besides, your Aunt Laura is sweet, and she can use my help."

*   *   *

At the end of March, Lisetta moved in with Ed and Ella, and Minnie moved in with Gus and Laura. The first day at suppertime, Gus tried to shock Minnie with a dirty joke, but she put him in his place. "Ach, du altes Schwein," she said. "Halt dein Mund."

Gus was taken aback. He sat sulking in silence throughout the remainder of the meal. The next day at suppertime, Gus quietly talked only about family and friends.

"I saw August Krueger at the saloon in Hoskins today," he said.

"Was he on a toot?" asked Minnie.

"No, at least not then."

"When he worked for us, he used to go off on a toot every now and then. He'd just leave his wife, who was deaf, poor thing, and go off by himself. Eventually he got so drunk, the police picked him up and put him in jail. When he sobered up, he called Gus.

(*Brubble* he called him.) *Brubble, come bail me aus. I'm sittin' in jail.* And Brubble went into town and bailed him out."

"Why didn't you just fire the old coot?"

"Gus liked him. You know Gus; he liked everybody. And August was always a good worker. When he worked, he worked hard; and when he drank, he drank hard."

While Minnie was coping with life on her brother's farm, Lisetta was coping with life in Aunt Ella's house. With Loretta married and Engie teaching in Wisner, Lisetta was the child of the household, someone for Aunt Ella to take care of, to boss, and to criticize. On Saturday, Aunt Lisetta came by to invite Lisetta to the movies.

"I can't forbid you to go," said Ella to young Lisetta, "but if you were Engie, I wouldn't allow you to see such trash." Lisetta discussed Aunt Ella's attitude with Aunt Lisetta as they walked to the theater.

"Why doesn't she ever let Engie do anything?" Lisetta asked her aunt.

"I don't know. Nothing is ever good enough for Engie. And nobody is ever good enough for Engie. Mark my words! Engie will end up an old maid schoolteacher!"

The next Saturday, Lisetta had a date with her old schoolmate and neighbor, Robbie Fenter. Aunt Ella greeted him coldly when he came to call for Lisetta. The following day, she said,

"Why do you want to go with that Robbie?" Lisetta did not answer.

"I'm going to have to have a talk with your mother about all of the running around you do." The next time Minnie came into Norfolk, Ella said to her, "You shouldn't let Zettie go here and there with this person and that. She'll become a regular street mouse."

"Squeak! Squeak!" retorted Minnie in a high voice.

When the semester was over at Norfolk Junior College, Lisetta did not wait for Minnie to tell her to get a job. She knew she had no other choice. Once again, she was fortunate. The teacher's position was open at District 60, the school she had attended as a child. She made an appointment to speak with Walt Fenter, the Chairman of District 60 School Board.

"We can't offer you more than you made at your last job, Lisetta," Mr. Fenter said. Times are even worse than they were two years ago."

"I understand, Mr. Fenter. I feel fortunate just to be considered for the job."

"You'd have thirty students and all eight grades. You'd need to work hard and be firm."

"I'm two years older now. Twenty instead of eighteen. The kids liked and respected me then, and I think they will now, too."

"I'm sure they did. Well, we want someone who understands farm kids, so good luck, Lisetta." He handed her the keys to the building. "Stop by the school this summer, and let me know if you'll need any supplies for the fall."

After the interview, Lisetta walked back to Minnie's farm, where they were temporarily living in the basement. She found her mother peeling potatoes in the basement.

"I got the job!" Lisetta exclaimed.

"Good! Remember when Pearl Sewell came to hear you read? She put Mrs. Boser in her place, the old sourpuss."

"Ja, and now I'm the teacher at District 60."

"Here, teacher, you finish peeling while I start the sausage."

As Lisetta peeled potatoes at the table, her mind went back to the first time she had peeled potatoes, when Mabel showed her how. Mabel had called her a princess. *I was a princess then*, thought Lisetta. *I lived in a big new house on a prosperous farm. Dad drove a brand-new black Buick. And now, look at us! Living in two rooms in a basement!*

Minnie had made the main room into a kitchen. In the center of the room were the kitchen table and chairs. Against one wall was a stove. On another wall were open shelves, where Minnie was storing her cooking supplies, pots and pans, dishes, and utensils. Along the third wall was a flight of stairs which led to the outdoors. On the fourth wall were double doors which led down a short flight of stairs into a fruit cellar. Off the main room was a second smaller room. The furnace was at one end of the room. The other end, Minnie had made into a bedroom.

There were only two small windows in the basement, both too high to see out of, shutting out the sun and the fresh air. Lisetta thought of all of the other disadvantages of living here in this humble environment: going outside to the outhouse; carrying water from the windmill through the barnyard, up the hill, and down the stairs to the basement; sharing a bed with her mother; feeling cooped up and alone, like a child again.

"You've got a hangdog look," observed Minnie.

"Ja. I don't know how I can bear it down here all summer long. I feel like I'm in a prison with no windows."

"There are two windows right up there, Zettie."

"Ja, too high to see out of, and too small to let in the light."

"If I can bear it down here in the basement this summer, you can bear it. You're younger, and you have your whole life ahead of you."

There was a knock at the door. Lisetta walked up the basement stairs, unlatched the door, and greeted Lyle. He invited her to go dancing at the pavilion tonight with Marcella and himself. Lisetta jumped at the chance to escape, at least for the evening. After Lyle left, she immediately began to get ready, knowing it would take several hours. She would have to make more than one trip to the windmill for enough water to wash her hair and to bathe. The water would need to be heated on the stove. And she had her supper to eat, the dishes to do, and her dress to iron.

At the pavilion, Lyle, Marcella, and Lisetta sat together at a table close to the edge of the dance floor. Lisetta looked around to see if Walter was there. She did not see him, but she saw his brother Dick. Midway through the evening, Dick asked Lisetta to dance. It was a slow two-step, making it easy to converse.

"I thought you were running a grocery store in Sholes," began Lisetta.

"I was until recently. My wife and I separated, and I'm living in Hoskins with my parents and Walt."

"Walt told me last November about Minnie. Did you ever find her?"

"Ja, I finally found her back in Chicago, but she didn't want any more to do with me."

"I'm sorry, Dick. It was nice of Walt to take care of the store for you while you were gone."

"He's been good to me. He helped me sell my store in Sholes, too. He has his realtor's license now, you know."

"No, I didn't know that. Did you get a good price for the store?"

"No, Zettie. You know what it's like now. No one has any money. I was just lucky to get it off my hands."

"What are you doing now, Dick?"

"I've opened up a grocery store in Hoskins, with a loan from Walt."

"Walt loaned you money?"

"Ja. Three hundred dollars. Almost all he had left. Families have to stick together in times like these, you know."

When the two-step was over, Dick escorted Lisetta back to her table. As she sat waiting for Lyle and Marcella to return, she thought about her conversation with Dick, about Walt's ambition in getting his realtor's license, his concern for his brother, and his financial help. The vocalist began singing, "Every little bird seems to whisper Louise; birds in the trees seem to twitter Louise. Each little rose tells me it knows I love you, love you." The band modulated into "Goodnight, Sweetheart." Lisetta had danced this with Walter last November. For a moment she thought he was coming towards her, but then she realized that it was Dick.

"Have the last dance with me, Zettie, and I'll take you home."

Lisetta whispered to Lyle and then stepped onto the dance floor with Dick. This time, Dick talked only about himself, but on the way home, the conversation again turned to Walter.

"Walt has been offered a job in a bank in Goodland, Kansas," said Dick. "He's accepted and will be leaving next week." Lisetta's heart dropped into the pit of her stomach.

"Did you hear what I said, Zettie?"

"I heard. Is he going alone?"

"Ja, I think so, but a certain young lady I know would very much like to go with him."

"Adeline?"

"That's the one. She's been chasing him like crazy since he got back from Sholes. Every time they go out, she's got the next date planned already."

"Do you think Walt will take Adeline with him?"

"He won't ask her to go, but she might just follow him out there."

"I hope not, for his sake."

"Why Zettie, do you still care for Walt?"

"What difference does it make? He doesn't care for me anymore. He hasn't even contacted me since he came back from Sholes."

"He didn't think you wanted to see him. He told me that you didn't seem to care that he would be gone."

"Really? It seemed the other way around to me. Does he really still care for me, Dick?"

"Why don't you find out for yourself, Zettie? Shall I give him a message from you?"

"Ja. Tell him that Lisetta Meritz wants to see him before he goes to Kansas."

"I will, and I'll bet you'll have a visitor knocking on your door in a day or two."

Lisetta went to bed excited. Her heart had moved from the pit of her stomach into her throat. She lay awake most of the night, imagining a scenario with Walter. What could she say to keep him from moving to Kansas? What would he say to her? Maybe he wouldn't even come to see her.

But Walter did come – the next evening after supper. Lisetta recognized the sound of his coupe coming down the lane and went outside to meet him.

"Dick said you wanted to see me before I leave for Kansas."

"Ja. Let's take a walk."

Lisetta directed Walter into a grove of tall cottonwood trees west of the house. The trees were still shedding their cotton, and the ground was almost white, as if it had been snowing. Lisetta looked up and saw the heart-shaped leaves shimmering in the sunlight. As the wind rustled through the trees, the leaves seemed to be saying, *speak*. Lisetta took a deep breath and spoke.

"Walt, I don't want you to go to Kansas."

"You don't? Why, Lisetta?"

"You know why, Walt."

"So, you do care for me after all."

"I've always cared for you, Walt. Even when we were just school kids, and you sat behind me at District 60."

"You were so chubby and cute, with your one braid hanging down your back."

"And you helped me read the assignments on the board that first day."

"And now we're both grown up."

"Ja, and I'll be the teacher at District 60 in the fall."

"You will, Lisetta? Good for you!"

"Ja. Ma is counting on my fifty dollars a month to help with the farm expenses."

"That's more than I'll be making at the bank in Kansas. I'll be making barely enough to support myself."

"Not enough to support Adeline as well?"

"Adeline isn't a girl to marry, Lisetta. She's not like you."

"Do you mean that, Walt?"

"You know I do. But I can't afford to do anything about it. I have just enough money left to get to Kansas."

"Don't go, Walt! Stay and work in Dick's store this summer. And in the fall, I'm sure you could pick corn on Emil's farm."

"And then when the winter comes? What then? There's not much for me here in Hoskins, Lisetta."

"There is, Walt! All the really important things: your family, your friends, your church. And me."

"And me with no permanent job. No, Lisetta, I can't stay here."

"I have a job, Walt."

"I know, Lisetta, but I have my pride. I wouldn't like to be supported by……

Lisetta interrupted. "There's an old saying, Walt: Faint heart never won fair lady."

"And you are a fair lady, Lisetta."

Walter took her in his arms and kissed her, and the cottonwood trees whispered, *stay*.

Lisetta went to bed with her mind reeling. She tried to remember her conversation with Walter verbatim, but her emotions kept interrupting her thoughts. Did Walter intimate that he would marry her if he had the money? Did he say that he loved her? Did he promise to stay? No, he didn't promise. He said something about pride.

The next day she was on tenterhooks, not knowing whether Walter would stay or leave. Tuesday and Wednesday crept slowly by. On Thursday, Minnie said, "Zettie, we're almost out of flour. Take the Buick into Hoskins and pick up a fifty-pound sack."

Lisetta jumped at the opportunity to go into Dick's store. On her drive into Hoskins, her mind raced. Would Walt be there? How should I act if he was? What if he wasn't there?

When she pulled up in front of the grocery store and looked through the window, she did not see Walter behind the counter. Nor did she see him when she walked through the door and looked around the store. Dick greeted her instead.

"Hi, Zettie! What can I get for you?"

"A fifty-pound sack of flour, Dick."

"All right, Zettie. I'll just get it from the back room."

Lisetta waited, downcast. Dick hadn't mentioned Walter. Then the door to the back room swung open, and Walter emerged with the sack of flour on his shoulder. Lisetta smiled and blushed.

"Where do you want this, Lisetta?"

"In the back seat, please. So, you haven't left for Kansas yet."

"I'm not going, Lisetta. You were right. The really important things are here."

"You won't be sorry, Walt. You'll see; everything will work out."

"We'll work it out, Zettie, together."

Early the next Saturday, Walter picked up Lisetta for an excursion to Waterbury to visit his brother Bill and his family. As they approached the District 11 schoolhouse three and a half miles east of Hoskins, Lisetta said,

"See that pasture on the right there? See the stream and bluff just beyond? That's where my Grandma Bech lived with her children in a dugout all winter after her husband died."

"She must have been very courageous."

"She was – a plucky pioneer. Just think, only sixty years ago, this was all prairie for as far as the eye can see."

"I know, and now it's full of farms and windmills and fences. I'd like to own some land someday, Lisetta. I know you'll inherit land, but I won't. I'll have to earn mine."

"You will, Walt. You're ambitious."

As they headed northeast towards Waterbury, the smaller hills gave way to big sweeping hills. Coming over the top of a rise, they saw on their left a cemetery with lush green grass. The graves had a view of the entire countryside below.

"That's the Pleasant View Cemetery," said Walter. "My parents will be buried there some day."

"And there's Winside down there," responded Lisetta. "How pretty it looks!"

Winside was located on the next sloping hill, the other side of the road. From this distance, they could see a stream below and a road leading over the bridge and into the town. The entire town was built on the south side of the hill, with the places of business at the bottom, the houses staggering up the hillside, and a water tower at the summit of the hill.

"Doesn't Adeline live in Winside?" asked Lisetta.

 Walter nodded but kept his eyes on the road. From Winside, the drive continued through the countryside and the towns of Wayne, Wakefield, and Emerson. They reached Waterbury just before noontime dinner. Bill and Ruby's six children were already seated around the table, the youngest just a toddler.

"You were just a baby, Lisetta, when I worked on your parents' farm," said Bill as they

sat down at the table. "Your mother used to tell me I was one of her favorites."

"You and Hank," responded Lisetta.

The conversation soon turned from family to politics.

"Did you read about the farmers in Iowa who have been picketing the roads?" Bill asked Walter.

"No, I haven't spent money on a paper recently. What were they picketing for?"

"To prevent the delivery of their grain and milk and livestock at such rock-bottom prices. I tell you, Walt, a farmer can't afford to produce anymore. President Hoover keeps telling us that prosperity is just around the corner, but the people in the bread lines don't believe it, and I'm tired of being one step away from a bread line."

"If we weren't living on the farm, we'd starve with all these kids," added Ruby.

"If you both can make it through this depression with six kids, Lisetta and I should be able to make it on our own," responded Walter, giving Lisetta a wink.

This time when Lisetta reached home, she was sure of Walter but afraid to tell Minnie. She decided to keep it a secret for a while, at least until they had set a wedding date. However, keeping such an important secret from Minnie made Lisetta feel emotionally estranged from her; and yet here she was, sharing a bed with her mother, being physically closer to her than she had been since she was a baby. Finally, towards the end of July, Lisetta could keep the secret no longer.

"Ma," she said, "Walt and I plan to marry at the end of August, right before the beginning of school." Minnie was not surprised.

"What will you live on, Zettie?"

"On my teacher's salary and any jobs Walt can get. This fall he'll pick corn on Emil's farm."

"I was counting on your financial help here on the farm, Zettie."

"We can all work together, Ma. The Getzmer family are pulling together in these hard times. We can do that, too."

"I suppose you'll want a church wedding and a white gown."

"Lyle and Marcella had a church wedding."

"All right. There's no harm in looking at wedding gowns."

Minnie and Lisetta drove into Norfolk on Saturday to look at gowns.

"They're so expensive!" exclaimed Minnie.

"Ja, I wish Uncle Harry were still in business in Norfolk."

"Well, their store is gone, the farm is gone, and their house is gone. Alles weg."

Lisetta felt guilty trying on gowns. Finally, holding the least expensive one, she said,

"I like this one best, Ma." The saleslady looked at Minnie.

"Let's wait," said Minnie. "I can't buy it today."

Several weeks later, Minnie said, "Zettie, I can't afford to buy you a wedding gown or give you a church wedding. You'll have to wait to get married. It doesn't have to be now when no one has any money. Wait until times are better. Be sensible!"

Lisetta could not go to her room and cry as she had done in the old days. So; she went outside, walked up the lane, crossed over a fence, and began running through the pasture. When she ran out of breath, she flopped down on the ground, just missing a musk thistle. She was tempted to pull it out of the ground and present it to Minnie as a gift.

That evening Lisetta and Walter discussed Minnie's decision and then made one of their own. They agreed to not wait indefinitely.

"Let's call Laura and Red," suggested Lisetta, "and ask them to meet us at the Bruce Pavilion on Saturday night. They have a secret marriage. Maybe they can help us with some plans."

During the course of Saturday evening, the two couples planned Walter and Lisetta's elopement. Teachers' convention would be held in Wayne in early October. Lisetta would attend the convention. Walter would meet her in Wayne. The two couples would drive to Elk Point, South Dakota, where Walter and Lisetta would be married by the same minister who had married Laura and Red, with the married couple as witnesses. After the ceremony, the two couples would drive to a hotel in South Sioux City, Iowa for a short celebration. The next morning, they would all return to Wayne. Laura and Red would go back to college, Lisetta would attend the convention, and Walter would drive home alone. And it would all remain a secret until later.

Chapter 13: Struggling together

By the end of the summer, Charlie Ohlund had the upstairs finished. Because Minnie had become accustomed to cooking in her kitchen in the basement, she seldom used her new upstairs kitchen. However, she enjoyed her new living room and the adjacent porch. Lisetta was elated that she could move back into a bedroom of her own. Minnie took the small bedroom at the top of the stairs. There were two larger bedrooms at the end of the hall, and Lisetta chose the cooler one, facing the lane. Although there was a bathroom on the second floor, it contained no fixtures. They still had to carry their water up the hill from the windmill and go outside to the privy.

In September, school started for Lisetta at District 60. As Mr. Fenter had told her, she had thirty students in grades one through eight. Although her class was almost twice as large as it had been at District 85, she found teaching easier. Her organizational and disciplinary skills had improved, and the curriculum was not new to her. She no longer needed to work out arithmetic problems each evening until bedtime.

Once again, she was determined to be a dedicated and caring teacher. She did not want any parents complaining about her to Pearl Sewell as Minnie had done when Lisetta was a student here. Early in the year, her dedication was put to a test. Ray Walker, one of her eighth-grade students, became ill with a kidney disease, forcing him to be bedridden for long periods at a time. To help him to keep up with his class, Lisetta walked to his home every other day to tutor him. Instead of turning west towards home at the T-junction, she walked a mile east towards Ray's. After the lesson, she backtracked to the T-junction and walked home, adding several hours and hundreds of steps to her day.

On her tutoring days, she got home just in time for supper, which Minnie had waiting in the basement. After dinner, Minnie embroidered on the front porch or in the upstairs kitchen. Occasionally, Lisetta entertained Walter in the parlor or in the dining room, but more often, they left the house so that they could discuss their future without fear of being overheard.

On Sunday, October 2nd, Lisetta drove Minnie's Buick to Wayne to attend the teachers' convention. She stayed with Laura that night at Neihardt Hall. The next day, when Walter arrived at noon, Lisetta left the convention, and the two couples headed for Elk Point.

When they reached Elk Point, they went directly to the county courthouse for a marriage license. Then they stopped at Woolworth's, where Walter purchased two cheap wedding bands. Lisetta tried hers on as Red headed for the parsonage next to the Presbyterian Church, where he and Laura had been married a year ago.

When they knocked promptly at seven-thirty, Reverend Bissell was waiting for them. After a brief introduction, the ceremony was underway – an invocation, the wedding vows, and a prayer. It was all over by seven-forty-five.

"Let's begin the rest of our lives," Walter whispered as he bent down to kiss Lisetta.

It was only a short distance from Elk Point to the hotel in South Sioux City, where Laura had made reservations for adjoining rooms. For an hour, the newlyweds joined Laura and Red in their room for a celebration. Mrs. Harmon had sent along with Laura four pieces of cake and a container of coffee.

"Isn't it wonderful to have such good friends?" Lisetta asked when she and Walter were finally alone.

"I don't think we could have eloped without them. But here we are, together forever."

"Come rain or shine, good times or ---

Walter kissed her before she could say *bad*.

By nine o'clock the next morning, Lisetta was back at Wayne for the second day of the convention. Walter kissed her good-bye and drove home to Hoskins in his coupe. At the end of the day, Lisetta motored home to the farm in the Buick, visited with Minnie a while about the convention, and went to bed alone.

During October and November, Walter continued to come over to see Lisetta each evening, as though they were still courting. Several times they were on the verge of telling Minnie their secret, but they always lost their nerve. Finally, one evening in late November, when Walter had picked the last of the corn at Emil's, he confessed.

"Mrs. Meritz, Lisetta and I were married on October 3rd, and we're tired of keeping it a secret." Minnie sat down in a chair for a moment.

"Well," she finally said, without emotion, "you might as well live together. Bring your things over, Walt, when you come for Thanksgiving dinner."

Lisetta was surprised at Minnie's civility. Perhaps, she thought, Ma likes Walt better now that he isn't a businessman. Or maybe she's just relieved that she doesn't have to pay for a church wedding and a gown.

In school on the following Monday, Miss Meritz suddenly became Mrs. Getzmer. At first her students were shocked; then they became restless, anxious to get home to relay the news of the elopement. The neighborhood was soon buzzing about it.

A week later, the news was old news. Lisetta and Walter settled into life together on Minnie's farm. Lisetta continued to walk to and from school each day, Walter continued to search for jobs or to help Dick in the grocery store or Emil on the farm, and Minnie continued to struggle to build up her farm.

Everything that she and Gus had possessed across the road, she had turned over to Lyle. She was proud of having set her only son up in farming. He was the beneficiary of the big two-story house with indoor plumbing, gas-powered washing machine, and large kitchen stove with warming closets and a hot-water reservoir; the poultry: the large flock of chickens, hens, roosters, pullets, and chicks, geese and ducks; the livestock: nine cows and calves, five horses, sixty hogs, twenty sows and piglets, and forty head of cattle; the farm equipment and machinery: the plows, harrow, disc, seeder, cultivator, hayrack, binder, grass mowers, stacker, hay sweeps, manure spreader, wagons, and hand implements; the farm buildings: the large three-sectioned barn with hayloft, hog barn, granary, blacksmith shop, machine shed, hen house, smokehouse, garage, hired hand's house; the established plantings: the garden, orchards, and groves of tall trees; and the well-maintained fences and roads. Finally, he was the beneficiary of the fifteen thousand dollars cash, which had been used for the livestock investment before the 1929 crash.

In contrast, Lisetta and Walter had nothing, and Minnie now had a smaller, less elegant house with no indoor plumbing, no washing machine, and a rudimentary cast-iron stove. She would have to build up her livestock and poultry from a few small purchases: three cows, two sows, a half-dozen laying hens. Minnie was fortunate that Gus had built a large barn with hayloft, hog barn, granary, and a smokehouse on her farm. But there had been no inhabitable house, no garage, and no hen house when she first moved back to the farm. And there was no garden – no fruits and vegetables all summer long, and none to can for the winter. Until she could prepare the soil, plant a garden, and build a fence around it, she would have to make do with the canned goods she had put up at 1208 Nebraska Avenue.

It was Monday, a washday. Minnie had carried bucket after bucket of water up from the windmill, enough to fill her large tubs. On a washboard, she scrubbed the soiled clothing with homemade soap. Then she boiled the clothes in a tub atop the cast-iron stove. With a stick, she lifted the hot clothes into another tub of cool water. She rinsed them, wrung them out, placed them in a clothes basket, carried them up the steps, and hung them outside on the clothesline. After the strong March wind had whipped them dry, she took them down from the line and carried them into the house to be sprinkled, rolled up, and covered, ready for ironing on Tuesday.

When Walter, Lisetta, and Minnie sat down to eat supper that Minnie had hastily prepared, Minnie was hot, tired, and irritable. Walter was out of sorts, too, the end of a fruitless day of searching for work.

"Did you have any success today, Walt?" asked Lisetta.

"None. I stopped by to see a few people, looking for leads. Saw Doc Brauer, Mr. Rohrke, and Mayor Bruce." He raised his hands in a hopeless gesture. "They knew of nothing."

"Something will turn up sooner or later. You'll see," encouraged Lisetta.

"I disagree," said Minnie. "I was able to give my son a good start in life. That's what you need these days."

Lisetta blushed at Minnie's rudeness. Walter sat quietly, studying his plate of food. "Mrs. Meritz" he finally said, "if I were your son, I would be ashamed to take all that you've given him and let you live the way that you're living now. You know, my mother is poor, but she at least has a hand-powered washing machine to wash her clothes in. I wouldn't let my mother use a scrubbing board."

Minnie had to have the last word. "Hard work never hurt anyone. But you, you'll have your feet under my table for the rest of my life!"

Walter immediately withdrew his feet from under her table, got up, and left the room. Lisetta followed him up to their bedroom. "Sorry," she said. "Ma can be that way at times. But she didn't mean it."

"I think she did. I'll tell you what, Lisetta, I'm going into Hoskins tomorrow to see my folks. Maybe I can make arrangements for us to live with them."

"How would I get to school?"

"There are only two months left before vacation. I'll drive you into the country each day."

"All right, Walt, if you think it's best."

A week later, they moved into the Getzmer's house. Walter had arranged it so that they had all of the privacy they wanted. Wilhelm and Emelia had already been accustomed to living in only a portion of their house: the kitchen, adjoining bedroom, pantry, and the back porch. By closing off the front part of the house, they saved the cost of heating it. So; Walter and Lisetta had a living room, dining room, and three bedrooms to use as they pleased, all humbly furnished.

Walter transformed the dining room into a kitchen. He purchased a small second-hand kerosene stove with two burners. A small portable oven, big enough for two loaves of bread or one pie, could be placed on top of one burner for baking. He cut a hole in the wall between their new kitchen and his mother's kitchen and hooked the stovepipes together.

When Lisetta stepped into their new living quarters for the first time, Walter had the table laid with two plates, two cups and saucers, and knives, forks, and spoons. On the stove stood one pot and one frying pan. In the portable oven were a bread pan and a pie plate.

"Oh, Walt!" exclaimed Lisetta. "I love it! Just think, our own home!"

"We'll have to share the outhouse with my folks and the basement when you do the laundry. But it's a beginning."

What a resourceful guy I married, thought Lisetta.

108

The elder Getzmers left the younger ones alone to adjust to married life. When there was contact between the two couples, the younger Getzmers instigated it. Occasionally, Lisetta knocked on the door and then walked through to Emelia's kitchen for some advice on cooking.

"Walt loves the way you cook chicken," she commented one Saturday morning. "Ma always fries young chicken, but you fix an older chicken so it tastes young and tender, he says."

"Ja. Start it early in zeh morning on zeh top of zeh stove und cook it all day. Put an onion inside, und sprenkel ein bisschen Pfeffer. By the time you eat, it falls off zeh bones."

Another time, Lisetta complained that there was no meat for dinner.

"Have you ein bisschen bacon?" asked Emelia.

"Ja, a little."

"Vell, fry it, und put fresh green beans und peas damit. Steam zem und

put over boiled potatoes. Valter loves it."

During April and May, money for food was scarce. When the school year ended, so did Lisetta's salary. One Sunday evening in early June, Dick dropped by to see them.

"How's business at the grocery, Dick?" asked Walter.

"Slower than molasses in January. There's too much competition for a small town. The old folks trade with old man Heberer, and a lot of the younger folks go to Norfolk. And now my stock is so low, there's nothing to buy even if folks do come in. I suppose you couldn't loan me some more money, could you, Walt?"

"No, I'm broke, Dick, but Lisetta and I could sure use the three hundred I loaned you already. It's a job putting food on the table these days."

"I'm sorry about the three hundred, Walt. But I do have an idea. Being single again, I can take off this summer and work in the wheat fields. If you like, you can have the store in payment for that three hundred. Maybe you'd make a go of it."

"What do you think, Lisetta?" asked Walter. "Should we try running a grocery store?"

"School's over for the summer. We could see how it goes." She paused. "Ja, I think it would be fun working together in a grocery store. We could use my May check from District 60 to stock the store."

The next morning, Walter and Lisetta walked to the store to look it over and make plans. It was located next to Heberer's Grocery on the left and an empty store on the right. Two low, empty windows faced the street, one on either side of the wooden door.

"We're going to keep something in those windows all the time," said Walter. "Whatever we've a lot of and want to get rid of or whatever we put on sale."

"Good idea," responded Lisetta.

They unlocked the door and entered a narrow room. Bare shelves lined the walls to the right and left of the door.

"And our shelves are going to look full even if they're not."

"How will we do that, Walt?"

"We move the canned and packaged goods to the edge of the shelves and leave space behind them instead of in front of them."

"How do you know so much about running a grocery store, Walt?"

"Experience. Remember, I took over Dick's store in Sholes when he was off looking for his wife."

"I remember. And you didn't write me."

Walter had moved over to the counter in the back of the store and pretended not to hear this comment.

"Come on, Lisetta. I'll show you how to work the cash register."

Walter demonstrated it to her.

"I'll have to get some rolls of coins from the bank in Norfolk and have enough dollar bills on hand to change a five-dollar bill, just in case someone rich walks in."

On top of the counter were a weighing scale, a meat cutter, and a cream tester.

"What's that?' asked Lisetta, pointing to the cream tester.

"That's a device for testing the percent of butterfat in the cream. When the farmers bring in their cream to sell, we'll test samples of it so that we can pay them according to how rich in fat the cream is."

"We'll pay them? I thought we would be selling items to them."

"We will. Here's how it works. They bring in their live chickens and their eggs and their cream, and we buy them. We keep the chickens in coops in the back room for several days and feed them wet mash. Then right before we take them to the produce store in Norfolk, we feed them cracked corn. They'll gobble up as much of the corn as their crops will hold, and we'll make money on the weight they've gained, as well as on the cream and eggs."

"Well, why wouldn't the farmers just take their own produce into Norfolk?"

"These are hard times, Lisetta. Driving to and from Norfolk takes time and gas. I can load everything onto my trailer and pull it behind the coupe. I'll take all the produce from several farmers at the same time and sell it. Then I'll stop at the wholesale house, buy goods, load them onto the trailer, and bring them back here to sell."

"That's smart," said Lisetta. "But what about prices? How will we know what to pay the farmers and what to charge for our goods?"

"That's where I need to do some research. I'll tell you what. Tomorrow I'll drive into Norfolk and go to some produce and wholesale houses and get prices and find out which ones we want to do business with. And I'll pick up some copies of The Norfolk Daily News. We'll study the ads to see what the grocery stores in Norfolk are charging for their goods."

"Good plan!"

"Do you want to come with me?"

"No. I'll stay here and get the store ready. I'll wash the windows and dust the shelves and the counter. The cooler needs cleaning inside, I noticed. And I'll scrub the floor. This place is dirty, too dirty for me to work in."

The next evening, Walter returned with all of the information he needed from Pilley's Produce. In addition, he had found a wholesale house that was willing to sell split cases of items.

"Here's their price list," he said to Lisetta as he walked into the house. "And here are the newspapers. Tonight, we'll study the prices and make a list of items to buy."

After supper, Walter and Lisetta sat down with the newspapers. Between the ads for the O. P. Skaggs Grocery, the U and I Store, and the Owl Grocery, they determined the going price for most of the items they planned to sell:

Bon Ton Flour	24 lbs.	89 cents
Sugar	10 lbs.	53 cents
Calumet Baking Powder	1 lb.	22 cents
Butternut Coffee	1 lb.	25 cents
Peanut Butter	1 qt. jar	23 cents
Post Toasties	3 packages	25 cents
Wheat Puffs	1 package	5 cents

Ivory Flakes	1 package	8 cents
White King Soap	10 bars	23 cents
Potatoes	10 lbs.	27 cents
Oranges	1 dozen	19 cents
Bananas	1 lb.	5 cents
Corn	No. 2 can	2 for 27 cents
Peaches	No. 2 ½ can	2 for 29 cents
Butter	1 lb.	23 cents
Cheese	1 lb.	19 cents
Ground Beef	2 lbs.	27 cents
Bacon	1 lb.	20 cents
Wieners	1 lb.	20 cents
Beef Roast	1 lb.	10 cents
Pork Roast	1 lb.	5 cents
Chicken	1 lb.	3 cents
Eggs	1 dozen	6 cents

While Lisetta was looking at prices of grocery items in the paper, she couldn't help noticing the prices of clothing: two women's dresses at Montgomery Ward's for $5; a pair of shoes for $1.95; spring coats $4.98; sweaters $1; men's suits $18.50.

Well, she thought, *at least we don't have to dress well to run a country grocery store.* She turned the page –

"Guess what's playing at the Granada," she said. Walter looked up from his paper.

"*Professional Sweetheart* with Ginger Rogers and Zasu Pitts. Admission: twenty-five cents."

"Twenty-five cents for you and twenty-five cents for me. That would buy ten pounds of potatoes and a quart jar of peanut butter."

"I know. Besides, we don't have time. We've got to figure out how many items of each product to buy and how much it will all cost. You give me the numbers, Walt, and I'll do the calculating."

The next morning, Walter drove to Norfolk to buy the wholesale goods. Lisetta stayed at home, cut up slips of paper, and labeled them with item and price. When Walter returned, they arranged the items on the shelves and attached the slips to the edges of the shelves with thumbtacks.

"Now we're ready," said Walter, standing back to look at the shelves, which appeared to be full but were actually almost empty.

"No we're not. We don't have a name for our store."

"Yes we do. Getzmer's"

"But we don't have a sign."

"Neither does anyone else in this town. But as soon as the customers step through that door, they'll see either you or me. And you don't look like old Mr. Heberer. You're a whole lot prettier."

*   *   *

By the end of the summer, Walter and Lisetta knew that they could make a living from the grocery store, a very humble, hard living. They kept the store open Monday through Saturday from eight o'clock in the morning until eight o'clock in the evening. On Sundays, Lisetta went to church in the morning, and Walter worked in the store until noon or until the last farmer had left.

Sunday was the day that the farmers stopped at the store to sell their chickens, cream, and eggs on the way to church. While they were in church, Walter tested the cream, weighed the chickens, and calculated the amount he could pay for their produce. After church, the farmers returned to the store to collect their money. The women shopped for food items they could afford to buy, leaving fifty cents for gas, enough to get home and back into Hoskins the next weekend.

After church one September morning, Lisetta hurried to the store to help Walter. When she arrived, Walter had just finished waiting on Irene Mittelstadt, who was leaving with big bags of groceries in her arms.

"That was a good sale," he said when Irene was out of earshot. "I wish more of the Hoskins ladies were married to mail carriers."

"Ja. The people with government jobs are the only ones who have money these days. Oh! Oh! Here comes Mrs. Feiler."

Walter grimaced. Mrs. Feiler entered, walked over to the shelves, picked up a can of corn and a can of peaches and brought them to the counter. She walked over and inspected a bunch of bananas.

"This one is too ripe," she said, pulling it off. She brought the bananas to the counter. Then she walked over to the potatoes and inspected them.

"They have too many sprouts," she said. "Do you have other potatoes?"

"I'll just check in the back," said Walter.

In the back room, Walter removed the sprouts from a half dozen potatoes and brought them out. "Here are some nice ones, Mrs. Feiler."

"I want a three-pound pork roast. Not too fat."

Walter took a roast from the cooler and weighed it. "Three pounds, two ounces," he announced.

"Trim that fat off there on that side."

Walter obeyed. "Three pounds, one ounce," he announced.

"There's still some fat there," she pointed.

Walter trimmed again. "Three pounds exactly."

Lisetta had been adding up the groceries. "Fifty-five cents," she said.

Mrs. Feiler paid, picked up her groceries, and left.

"You should go into her husband's lumber store," she said to Walter, "and ask him to saw off a board inch by inch."

Walter did not have a chance to respond to this comment.

"Here comes your mother," he said.

"Zettie," Minnie said as she entered the store, "your Aunt Clara and Uncle Henry will be at the farm on Wednesday if you want to see them. They're making a trip from Fullerton."

"Thanks, Ma. I'll try to get out."

Minnie headed for the door.

"Need any groceries, Mrs. Meritz?" Walter called after her.

"No!" retorted Minnie. "I go to Norfolk for my groceries. Hoskins gets my dust!" She walked out, letting the screen door bang.

"Too bad we can't charge for dust," quipped Walter to Lisetta.

Chapter 14: Parenting

One Sunday afternoon in September of 1933, Walter and Lisetta were sitting on the front porch swing at the Getzmer acreage. Emelia and Wilhelm's dog Shep sat at their feet. Shep was a big, mangy-looking dog, whose legs were a little too lanky and whose feet were a little too big for his body.

"Shep is a nice dog," said Lisetta, "but he sure is a Schlupps." Walter nodded and continued to read *The Norfolk Daily News.* "The paper says that $150,000 should be coming our way soon by the federal government."

"Our way?"

"Well, not yours and mine. Aid to the farmers. You know, from the AAA, the Agricultural Adjustment Act passed in May in Congress."

"If the farmers get aid, they'll be able to buy more. It'll help us, too, Walt."

"Ja, and the Beer-Wine Revenue Act should help the economy, too. It states

here that they're already selling beer and wine legally in Madison."

"I'll bet it'll be just a matter of time before prohibition is repealed."

"Ja. President Roosevelt campaigned that he would put a chicken in every pot.

I guess that includes liquor."

"I wish he'd do something about the banks. It's so inconvenient to have to go to Norfolk for a roll of nickels," complained Lisetta.

"Well, the Hoskins Bank wasn't big enough to make the national keep list when Congress passed the Emergency Banking Relief Act."

While Lisetta and Walter had been visiting, the sky had gradually gotten darker and darker with big, black thunderclouds. A storm was approaching from the west. In the distance, they could hear the low rumble of thunder, like someone playing kettledrums beyond the hills on the horizon. Shep began to whimper.

"Shep's afraid of storms," said Walter. There was a flash of lightning in the western clouds and another east of that and then a series of flashes as though the clouds were engaged in a heated dialogue. Suddenly, there was a clap of thunder so loud that the windows in the house rattled.

"Ooh!" screamed Lisetta. Shep tore off the porch, with his tail between his legs, and raced around the side of the house towards the back while huge drops of rain splattered down upon him. Walter laughed.

"He's headed for the back door. He knows how to open it. In a minute, he'll be hiding under the folks' bed."

"What a funny Schlupps he is," Lisetta repeated.

"We better get inside," Walter said, arising from the swing.

"Just a minute, Walt, before we go in. I wanted to tell you – I may be pregnant."

Walter sat down and took her hand. "Are you worried, Lisetta?"

"No, Walt, I'm happy. I'd like a baby. But we're so poor."

"I'd like one, too" He pulled Lisetta up from the porch swing and gave her a big hug.

"Don't worry about the money. We can manage somehow, Honey."

By their first anniversary on October 3rd, Lisetta was certain. The baby would be born sometime in late May or early June. When Lisetta told Minnie about it, she said, "Lyle and Marcella are going to have a baby, too. In March."

"Good! Then our children will be close in age."

"I told Lyle, and I'm telling you now, I'm giving you each a crib. But that's all. The rest is up to you."

 When Lisetta reported this conversation to Walter, he said, "We'll manage to get what we need for the baby, but I 'm concerned for my parents. I'm afraid the baby will cry and disturb them. They're old now. They've raised a big family, and they deserve their peace and quiet."

"I agree," responded Lisetta. "Besides, I don't think I could manage the laundry here. You know, those steps into the basement are steep and treacherous. And that old vacuum-powered washing machine down there – imagine washing all those diapers by pushing the handle back and forth, back and forth."

"We need to look for a house to rent, and buy ourselves a modern washing machine. I'll start enquiring if anyone needs a renter," promised Walter.

*　　　*　　　*

All winter long, they hunted for a house they could afford, a small house, one within walking distance of the store. Finally, towards the beginning of April, they heard that old Mrs. Pfeil wanted to rent out her house and move back to the country.

Walter and Lisetta went over to look at it. The one-story frame house had a steep roof with an attic window in a single gable. There were four rooms: a living room with a pot-bellied stove; to the right of the living room, a small bedroom; to the back, the kitchen; off the kitchen, a small pantry and a second bedroom.

"There's no stove in the kitchen," Lisetta said to Walter. "Our little two-burner one won't do when the baby comes."

"I know. We'd have to buy one."

They stepped through a door from the kitchen to an enclosed porch on the south side of the house.

"We could put a washing machine out here," suggested Lisetta.

"But there's no running water."

"Look! There's a pump." Lisetta pointed. "I wouldn't have far to carry the water. And look! There's a cave for storing fruit and vegetables."

Lisetta walked back into the house and into the front bedroom. From the side window, she could see into the beautiful bay window in the dining room of the former Bech house across the street. She remembered the little doggie bed that Grandma Bech had always kept in that room, and when she visited, she ran in, picked up the little white poodle and smothered him with kisses.

"A penny for your thoughts," said Walter, coming up behind her.

"My Grandma and Grandpa Bech used to live across the street there when they retired from the farm."

"Oh, that's nice for you. Good memories. What do you think? Shall we take the house?"

"Can we afford a washing machine and a cookstove?"

"Ja. Just."

A month later, Walter and Lisetta were invited to a family celebration following the baptism of Lyle and Marcella's baby. During the dinner afterwards, Lyle asked Walter, "How's the store going, Walt?"

"We're doing all right. We have some steady customers now. We'd like to have your business, though, Lyle."

"Well, you know, we go to Norfolk for our groceries. I always have some other business to attend to there."

"You'll rot in that grocery store," added Minnie. "The better class of farmers will never trade with you."

Lisetta frowned at her mother and changed the subject.

"We're all settled in our house. I have a new gas-powered washing machine, and I am ready to wash lots and lots of diapers."

The conversation turned to names for babies, and Lisetta explained that she and Walt hadn't yet decided on a girl's name but had agreed on "Gus" if the baby was a boy.

On a Sunday afternoon in May, Walter and Lisetta were invited out to Minnie's farm to pick strawberries. As they were driving through Hoskins with the windows rolled down, they could smell the sweet perfume of the lilac bushes growing in people's yards. The tall bushes were loaded with sprays of blossoms, the new blossoms still lilac in color, the older blossoms almost white. When they got to the farm, they found more lilac bushes blooming along the fence in Minnie's garden.

"Isn't that a heavenly smell?" asked Lisetta as she stooped to pick a few berries. She was so heavy with child, she could barely stoop.

"Let me do this, Lisetta," offered Walter. "You go inside and wait for me."

Lisetta went into the parlor, took out some sheet music from the piano bench, and sat down to play and sing.

"I'm in heaven when I see you smile. Smile for me, my Diane," she sang.

No, she thought, *she'd be called "Di" and I hate it when I'm called "Li."*

After playing "Charmaine, My Sweet Charmaine" and "Ramona," she began singing, "Jeannine, I dream of lilac time. Your eyes, they beam in lilac time."

Lisetta stopped singing, remembering the aromatic lilacs. She ran out to Minnie, who was embroidering on the porch. "Ma, do you like the name *Jeannine?*"

"Jeannine? Jeannine. Ja, I like that."

"That's it, Ma. I'll call the baby Jeannine if Walt agrees."

On Monday, June 4th, the little lilac started to bloom. At noon Lisetta's water bag broke. Dick was helping out at the store, and when Walter came home for dinner at twelve-thirty, Lisetta reported her condition.

"I'll walk back to the store and call Doc Brauer," he said excitedly.

Jeannine was born at ten-thirty in the evening. Eight pounds, eight ounces. Minnie came over the next day to see her. Taking the baby in her arms, she said, "What a beautiful baby! Kleine Jeannine. Jeannine Francis - Getzmer" she added, her voice slightly subdued.

*   *   *

All summer long, Dick helped Walter at the store while Lisetta stayed home with Jeannine.

Walter was reading the paper during a spare moment in late September. "Look at this headline!" he said to Lisetta: LINDBERGH KIDNAPPER CAUGHT.

"Oh, good! They finally caught him!"

"Ja, but the baby hasn't been returned."

"I can't imagine how the Lindberghs must feel. Just think how we'd feel if our baby were kidnapped. I guess that we're lucky we're not rich and famous city folks."

"Speaking of riches, we are about to become poorer. According to the paper, the O.P. Skaggs Grocery has dropped their prices again. Listen to this: potatoes, fifteen pounds for twenty-nine cents; ground beef, two pounds for seventeen cents. How can we ever make a profit? Things just keep getting worse."

By Christmastime, Dick was gone again, and Lisetta was back working part-time in the store. She brought Jeannine along in her carriage and stayed until the baby was too fussy to handle. One of her frequent customers now was Minnie, who came in to purchase a few items at a time and stayed to play with Jeannine.

"Look at this paper," Minnie said, breezing through the door and handing it to Walter.

"What am I supposed to see?" Walter asked.

"That article on the AAA. As of the end of November, the federal government has given over $506 million to the farmers. I tell you, Walt, you're in the wrong business. You need to get back on the farm where you can make a decent living for yourself and your family."

Walter did not respond. Mrs. Feiler had just entered the store, and he knew that she would demand special cuts of meat for the Christmas holiday.

Walter and Lisetta closed the store on Christmas Eve and Christmas Day, and Walter attended church for the fist time in over a year. They closed again for New Year's Eve and New Year's Day. They hired a baby-sitter and went to dance at the Bruce Pavilion in the evening and drove to Norfolk the next afternoon to see Jack Benny in "Transatlantic Merry-Go-Round" at the Granada Theater.

On the way home from the matinee, Lisetta remarked, "It's been a lovely holiday!" Walter nodded.

"Walt, I didn't want to tell you until the holiday was over. I think I'm pregnant again."

"Are you sure?"

"Pretty sure. I know it's too soon to have a second baby. Jeannine will still be a baby at the end of August."

"We can handle it. We could call the baby "August" or "Augusta" in honor of your relatives and mine."

Fauneil Ruth was born at home at nine o'clock on Sunday morning, August 25th.

"Just in time to go to church," Walter joked.

In the coming months, Lisetta found that with two babies, she could no longer work in the grocery store. For a while, Dick helped out. But in October, he left to pick corn, and Walter was on his own, tied down twelve hours a day. When he got home in the evening, Lisetta handed him either a diaper or a bottle for Jeannine while she attended to Fauneil.

Time and money were at a minimum. With two babies to feed, Walter and Lisetta could not afford to heat their four-room house. When the cold weather started, they closed the door to the living room and the front bedroom so that they wouldn't have to feed the pot-bellied stove. They moved their bed, Jeannine's walnut crib and Fauneil's tiny white crib into the very small bedroom off the kitchen. The big cookstove kept both the kitchen and the adjoining bedroom warm.

Minnie came often to visit, to give Jeannine the attention she felt she was missing. One day close to Christmas, she came to the house and found a quarantine sign posted on the door. She knocked, but there was no answer. She walked across the street to the former Bech house, but there was no answer there, either. She crossed the street to the Feiler's house.

"There's a quarantine sign on my daughter's door," she said when Mrs. Feiler answered the doorbell.

"Yes. They have scarlet fever over there."

"Ach, Gott in Himmel! All of them?"

"No. So far only the little baby has scarlatina."

"I suppose the grocery store is closed."

"Yes, Walt is quarantined, too, until Dr. Brauer is sure that the disease won't spread."

In a few weeks, Dr. Brauer pronounced the baby better and lifted the quarantine for the house and the store. The family was well, and they resumed their daily activities. Minnie remarked when she visited, "Thank God no one died from it. I bet Walt picked up the scarlet fever germs from someone who came into the store, and he brought them home."

Little Jeannine began clamoring for her grandma's attention. Minnie picked her up and continued the conversation. "Zettie, I wish you'd leave the store and take up farming. You know, all of our people have lived off the land, even before they came to this country. Why, your great great grandfather, Lorentz Christian Bech, was a shepherd in the seventeen hundreds."

"I know. Farming is a good life," Lisetta remarked.

"I've been thinking. If you and Walt wanted to farm, I could move across the road into the hired hand's house that your father built. It's empty now. You and Walt could take my house and rent my land – share rent. Three-fifths of the crops you raise for you, two-fifths for me. Of course, I would want to run my cattle in the pasture, and I need the hog barn for my hogs. But you could have my chickens and the hen house and the coops."

When Walter came home, Lisetta discussed Minnie's proposal with him.

"I don't know," he said. "We'd need capital to start out in farming, but do we really want to be tenants on your mother's farm?"

"I think Ma would be fair. It might be a better life. We're so tied down with the store."

"You're right. And I do miss farm life."

"If we could sell the store for enough money, we could buy a little stock and some machinery."

A month later, Walter had sold the store to young Ruben Weier for five hundred dollars. Ruben would take over at the end of February, prior to planting time.

The last week of February, Walter was working in the store when a stranger entered.

"I'm Art Post," he said. "I'm with the Rain and Hail Bureau of Omaha, in charge of the Nebraska, Colorado, and Iowa region."

"How do you do? I'm Walt Getzmer, owner of this grocery store."

"Walt, you must know the people around here pretty well."

"Sure do."

"I'm looking for a young man to adjust hail losses, someone with farming experience. Anyone you could recommend?"

Walter reflected a moment.

"Mr. Post," he said, "you might be looking at him right now." Art Post smiled. "I like your drive. I'll stop by and talk with you again in the spring before the hail adjusting season is underway."

"I won't be here, Mr. Post. I'm moving my family back to the farm for a better life. But when you come back to town, ask anyone. They'll tell you how to find me."

Chapter 15: On the Farm

The night before the move to the farm, Lisetta dreamed of a better life. In her dream, it was morning. She crawled out of bed, dressed, and crossed the hall to the bathroom, where she washed her hands and face and studied it in the mirror, - a pretty face, a hopeful face. She walked down the stairs to the kitchen and opened the cupboard to prepare breakfast. It was crammed full of Jersey Cream Pancake Flour, Butternut Coffee, Wheat Puffs, and Post Toasties. She reached for the Post Toasties. Some strawberries from the garden would be nice with this, she decided. She walked out into the yard. Flocks of chickens and ducks and geese were scampering about. She shooed her way to the garden, which was bursting with green beans, beets, peas, sweet corn, lettuce, radishes, and green onions, making it difficult to get to the strawberries.

While she was picking the berries, she heard a noise on the other side of the fence. She walked up to the fence, parted the branches of the lilac bushes growing alongside, and peeked over. Hank was there, trying to pick the corn, but it was so tall, he couldn't reach the ears. She called to him, but he didn't hear. He kept on reaching, reaching. She walked down the hill to the barn to search for something; she couldn't remember what. The barn was full of hay and horses, milk stools, a separator, wagons, and (she remembered what she had been looking for), a big black Buick.

She walked out of the barn and through the barnyard, through hogs and cattle, hundreds of them, and sows reclining next to the fences, their piglets suckling. She passed the windmill whirling round and round and climbed a fence into a prairie meadow. She stooped to pick a deep-pink prairie wild rose.

She looked up to see a herd of cattle grazing on the hillside, all facing up toward the top of the hill. Looking behind, she saw a line of cows in single file. Behind the cows was a bull, a big brown Hereford bull, angry, menacing. Suddenly he was charging at her. Move legs! Move!

The alarm rang, and Walter nudged her. "Wake up, honey. It's moving day."

They had little to move: a bed, dresser, two cribs, table and chairs, stove, washing machine, kitchen items, and clothes. While Lisetta stayed behind with the babies, Walter and Dick moved the household items with a small trailer, making several trips to the farm. Minnie was already settled across the road in the hired hand's house.

During the next week, Walter purchased animals and equipment, retaining several hundred dollars for living expenses. He and Lisetta agreed to the barest necessities: a team of horses, three cows, two sows, a wagon, plow, disc, and hand implements. The other farm equipment he planned to borrow from his brother Emil.

As the spring unfolded, Walter and Lisetta got the "better life" underway. Lisetta cared for the children and the house, tended the chickens, fed the livestock, milked the cows, and planted the garden. Walter plowed and planted corn and oats. At first, their future looked rosy. With the heavy snows during the winter and the April rains, the crop promised to be plentiful.

But during the month of May, the rains were scattered and short. And in June and July, there was no rain at all. When the oats were harvested, there was not enough to sell. Walter gave Minnie her share of the meager crop and stored his share in the granary, to be used for feed.

The corn struggled to survive. It sent down its roots deeper and deeper into the subsoil, searching for water. The edges of the leaves turned brown, and the leaves began to turn inward in an effort to protect themselves from the hot sun. Lisetta and Walter watched the sky each day for signs of rain. One evening, Lisetta saw streaks of light in the sky on the western horizon.

"The sun is drawing water," she said.

"That's ridiculous!" responded Walter. "The sun can't draw water."

"I know it. That's just an old expression, meaning it's going to rain."

"I doubt it. We've had thunder and lightning all summer, but never any rain."

Lisetta was right. That night it rained. It came down in torrents, pounding against the roof of the house, sheeting against the windowpanes. Lisetta and Walter went to bed, dreaming of green pastures and revived cornfields. But the next morning, they found the cornfields almost completely destroyed. The rain had beaten down the leaves and had made furrows in the ground, running along these into the ditches; the ground was too dry to drink in the moisture. Only along the edges of the furrows and in the low spots was there any chance for the corn now. In the afternoon, Walter said to Lisetta,

"There's nothing to do in the fields. I'm going to take my trailer into Hoskins and see about purchasing some scraps of lumber at Feiler's.

"What for, Walt?"

"To build a shelter for the hogs in the hay manger. They'll need it this winter."

Close to suppertime, Walter returned with the wood and the news.

"Emil's crop is all washed out, as bad as ours. But at least he still has his land. Poor Ferd has nothing left – no crops and no source of income. He will have to give up his land and work as a hired hand for Emil."

"You Getzmer boys sure have the bad luck, at least lately," commiserated Lisetta.

After two rainless weeks, Walter turned the cattle into the cornfields to eat the stalks before they completely dried up. By the end of August, the cattle had eaten all of the stalks, and there was nothing more in the fields for them to eat: no oats, no corn, no pasture, no prairie flowers, not even edible weeds.

"What are we going to feed our livestock, Walt? Lisetta asked. "We'd better not buy any feed. We'll need our cash for ourselves," she added.

"I've discussed it with Emil. We can feed the thistles to the cattle if we doctor them up, and I have an idea of my own for the pigs."

Walter drove into Hoskins and purchased some gallons of sorghum from the feedstore. When he returned, he dug a large ditch in the hay manger. Then he went out into the fields, pitched the thistles onto his wagon, and unloaded them into the ditch. Using the pitch fork, he broke them up as best he could and poured water and sorghum onto them. Then he opened the gate to allow the cattle access to the ditch and stood back, watching as they munched on the sweetened thistles.

"Smarty!" said Lisetta. "What's the idea for the pigs?"

"You'll see," he answered.

He hitched the trailer onto the coupe and drove into Norfolk to Pilley's Produce, where for pennies, he purchased moldy fruit, wilted vegetables, and rotten eggs. When he got back to the farm, he mixed some of them together in the pig trough, added a little water, and then stood back to watch them enjoy their meal.

"Clever!" praised Lisetta. "But it sure stinks! I'm glad I don't have to eat that concoction!"

"By the end of the week, it will be even smellier. I got enough for the whole week, and next week, I'll go back and get some more."

"Yum, yum. Lucky pigs."

Pilley's Produce remained a source of food for the pigs, but the cattle did not fare as well. When the thistles were all gone, Walter had to determine their fate.

"We can purchase enough hay to see the milk cows through the winter," he said. "We must have milk for the girls and for ourselves. But we can't keep the rest of the cattle. I'll butcher a steer so we'll have meat to smoke and can. The other two steers and the heifers I'll have to take to the auction house and sell for whatever I can get. Probably peanuts."

"How will you get them to the auction house?"

"Emil's truck. He'll be glad to help me."

*　　　*　　　*

Walter and Lisetta needed to prepare food for themselves for the winter – with Emil's help again. He came over and participated in butchering a steer and a pig. Lisetta ground the meat for the sausages and cleaned the intestines. Then they all worked furiously to stuff the intestines before the meat spoiled. They hung the hams and the sausages in the smokehouse and started a smoldering fire which they carefully tended in the coming weeks until the meat was thoroughly smoked through. Meanwhile, they prepared the meat for canning before it spoiled: cutting chunks of beef and pork, stuffing them into jars, baking the jars in the oven, and then sealing them with rubbers and metal lids.

"Well, we have meat now," said Lisetta when it was all done.

"Who knows what the winter will bring," answered Walter

The winter brought the north wind and subzero temperatures and snow and more snow. By December, the snow had imprisoned the entire countryside. Roads were impassable, even with a team of horses. The wind had whipped across the tops of the hills and had carried the snow into the valleys. And then more snow fell, and the wind drove the fresh snow onto the old drifts. At the bottom of the hills, the drifts stood eight feet high.

The farmers in the neighborhood contacted each other by telephone, making a pact to clear the roads by Christmastime. Those who had tractors attached scoops to them and scooped the snow with these while others used their shovels to scoop by hand. They worked together, creating one tunnel after another. The road tunnels they built were only wide enough for one vehicle, but at the bottom of each hill, they dug an additional crosspiece tunnel so that when two vehicles met each other, one could back into the crosspiece and wait while the other proceeded.

In addition to clearing the roads, each farmer had to scoop tunnels on his own farm in order to tend to his livestock. Walter had just finished digging his tunnels when he saw Minnie walking towards him through the deep drifts early one morning.

"Walt, can help me out?" she enquired. "I have a herd of cattle on that forty-acre section of mine. I haven't been able to get any hay over to them. Can you hitch the hayrack to your team and carry a load over to them?"

"I can't get a hayrack through the road tunnels. They're not wide enough."

"Then you'll have to go across the fields. Take down enough fence to get the rack through. We can rebuild the fences later when the snow has melted."

It took Walter a week to complete this mission of mercy. He took the team out each day and plowed through the snow, taking down fences along the way, and returning home each night. After he had cleared a path the entire way to the forty acres, he pitched hay from the barn onto the hayrack, hitched it to the team, and hauled the hay to the starving animals.

During this week, Lisetta tended to all of their own livestock. In the early morning hours, she waded through three feet of snow down the hill towards the barn. At the bottom of the hill, where the snow was deeper, she crept through the cold, icy tunnel that Walter had dug, milked the cows in the barn, ran the separator, and brought back the milk and cream to the house. After breakfast, she scooped the snow away from the hen house door, fed the chickens, and gathered the eggs. In the afternoon, she again waded through the snow to a second tunnel and then crept through it to feed the pigs in the hay manger.

At the end of the day, Walter and Lisetta were exhausted. "Who knows, maybe all of this snow is actually a blessing," said Walter, trying hard to console Lisetta, who was too exhausted to reply. "At least the ground should be plenty wet for spring planting," he added optimistically.

But the snow had no intention of being a blessing. It all melted in a bizarre February thaw, at a time when it was too early to plant. March followed with its typical strong winds, but it brought no snow, no moisture. April brought hope. There were enough showers to soften the earth so that the crops could be planted.

Before Walter had a chance to start the spring planting, he had a visitor. Art Post drove onto the farmyard early one evening.

"Remember me, Walt? I told you I'd look you up."

"I remember you, but I was expecting you a year ago."

"A year ago, there weren't many crops to adjust. Just enough for the adjustors we already had on board."

"Ja, we dried out here."

"Well, they've had good rains in Southern Nebraska and Kansas this spring. We're anticipating more work. Still interested, Walt? The pay is ten dollars a day, with all expenses on the road paid."

"That's good pay. Excellent pay. But I wouldn't want to be gone from my family more than a week or two at a time."

"We could work that out."

"When do you need someone?"

"Right away. Training starts next week in Omaha."

"I haven't planted my crops yet, Mr. Post. I have to get the oats and corn in."

"Hire someone, Walt. If you're making ten dollars a day with us, you can afford to pay farm wages."

"I don't know. Can you give me a couple of days to think it over?"

"Yes. Talk it over with your wife. We need men whose wives are willing to manage on their own."

After Art Post had left, Walter and Lisetta discussed the job offer and all that it entailed: the extra money, the traveling for Walter, and the added responsibility at home for Lisetta.

"I can handle my usual chores and supervise," said Lisetta, "but I can't work in the fields."

"I know. We would need to hire a man. I'll drive into Hoskins tomorrow, if you like, and find out if anyone around here is looking for farm work."

"Okay. If you find someone you know and can trust, go ahead and hire him. He can sleep in the furnace room in the basement, where Ma and I slept the summer before we were married."

Late the next afternoon, Walter came home excited.

"I found someone who can begin work immediately. I can get him started on the planting before I leave for Omaha."

"Well, who is it, Walt? Do I know him?"

"Ralph Lindquist."

"What? That bully who used to step on my toes at school? How could you?"

"I didn't know he stepped on your toes."

"Ja, and he called Rosie and me fat cud-chewing cows."

Walter laughed.

"Well, you can put him in his place now. After all, you're the boss when I'm gone, and he'll be sleeping two floors below you in the basement."

By the time Walter came back from his training session, Ralph had finished planting the oats; he was polite to Lisetta, and treated her as the boss.

"You seem happy, Walt. Are you going to like this job?"

"Yes, I'm learning a lot. So far, I've learned all about different crops at different stages of growth."

"Did they take you into the fields?"

"Ja, first we studied plants on film, showing different levels of damage. Then we went into the fields, and they demonstrated how to assess the damage from wind, rain, and hail. After a storm, a team of adjusters is sent to an area to adjust all of the crops in that area. You get a better assessment that way. We take samples from different parts of the fields – each of the corners and the center."

"A lot of walking then."

"You bet. It's hard work."

Walter was home long enough to get Ralph started on the corn planting. They had just finished the first day of planting when Art Post called. He was sending Walt to the Topeka area of Kansas for a two-week trip. "Bring some good, tall walking boots," he suggested.

*   *   *

When Walter returned several weeks later, he was browned from the sun and exhausted. He explained that it had been hard work: up at five in the morning, breakfast and out in the fields by six-thirty, walking a field and making an assessment to the farmer, driving to the next field; then lunch at a greasy spoon, working another field until dusk, dinner at another greasy spoon, writing up reports until bedtime.

"And you like that?" questioned Lisetta.

"Well, not the greasy spoon part. Can't wait for the roast beef and gravy I smell cooking. But, look, I made one hundred and ten dollars this trip."

"Walt, that's a lot of money."

"Ja, but my coupe conked out, and most of it will have to go towards a new car."

*   *   *

When Walter came home from a trip to Beatrice in late July, Ralph greeted him with the news that one of the horses was sick. Walter followed him to the barn, where he found the horse lying down in its stall. He called the vet immediately, who examined the horse and diagnosed encephalitis.

"Oh, my God!" exclaimed Lisetta. "Your sister-in-law died from that. Are our children safe?"

"Very little danger, but keep them away from the barn and from mosquitoes and ticks."

"Can you save the horse?" Walter asked.

The vet explained that he had given the horse a shot, but that the real danger was the sleeping part of the sickness. The animal had to be kept up and awake. The horse had to be raised with a rope and a sling put under it. Once the horse was up, it needed to be doused with buckets of cold water to keep it awake and to bring its temperature down. He added that if the horse stayed awake for the next three days, it had a good chance of pulling through.

128

Once again, Emil came to help out, bringing Ferd along with him. With the strength of Walter's brothers, Ralph, and himself, they pulled the horse up with a rope, put its legs through a hole they had cut in a canvas, slung the canvas under its belly, and tied the corners of the canvas to the four corner posts of the stall. Then Walter and Ralph took turns dousing the horse with water for three days. Fortunately, the horse survived. However, Emil lost his horse a short time later.

When Walter returned from another trip, Emil greeted him with the bad news. His horse had eaten poisoned bran that he had spread in his fields because of grasshoppers in Iowa which were heading west. He recommended that Walt go to the feedstore in Hoskins, purchase the bran, spread it, and carefully keep his animals from eating it.

On Sunday after the church service, Walter asked Mr. Rohrke what he remembered about the plague of Rocky Mountain locusts in the 1870's:

"I was just a young boy then" he relayed. "But I remember it as though it happened yesterday. We thought it was going to rain because the western sky turned black. But there wasn't any thunder or lightning. Then we heard a faint whirring noise. It got louder and louder. It sounded like airplanes coming, but there weren't any airplanes or automobiles back then. All of a sudden, the locusts were all around us – in our hair, on our faces, in our clothes, crawling up my pants and down my shirt. We ran for the dugout as fast as we could. How long we stayed there, I don't' remember, but when we went outside, what a sight!"

"All the vegetation was gone?" questioned Walter.

"Ja, every plant. Every leaf. Every weed. They even stripped the bark off the trees. The ground was covered with dead locusts six inches thick, for as far as the eye could see."

"How did they die?"

"They killed themselves. They crashed into each other and fell to earth."

"I guess I don't know much about locusts or grasshoppers," said Walter. "The ones I've experienced have been solitary creatures, quietly minding their own business."

"That's their normal state," explained Doc Brauer, who was standing nearby.

"They can become warlike, like a big army on the move."

"What makes their behavior change?"

"Crowding. Changes in climate. If there is plenty of rain and crops, they spread out over large areas, each one living by himself. But if a drought comes, they crowd together in the greener areas. The crowding makes them restless and irritable, and all it takes is a hot day to spark them into flight. They don't know where they're headed. They just keep flying until their body temperature changes, from a sudden drop in temperature or nightfall. And then they land!"

"It doesn't sound like we have much chance against them if they fly our way," said Walter.

"It all depends how many come."

The Hoskins community was as ready as they could be, but the grasshoppers did not come right away. In mid-August, Art Post called Walter to go on a two-week trip to Eastern Colorado. While he was gone, the grasshoppers came at night, and no one knew they were there until the next morning. Ralph came in to breakfast and announced that the ditches and the cornfield were full of dead grasshoppers.

"Is there any corn left?" asked Lisetta.

"About half of it has been eaten. There are a lot of dead ones from the poisoned bran, and a lot of the swarm was probably killed along the way."

When Walter returned, Lisetta met him with the news.

"What next," he responded. "Do you realize that since we moved onto the farm, we've experienced drought, a severe winter, torrential rain, sleeping sickness, and now grasshoppers."

Lisetta broke into deep sobs, her spirit broken. Walter held her tightly, trying to comfort her.

"Well, at least we have half of the corn left," he added in an attempt to be positive.

The struggle continued. There had been no rain for eight weeks. By September, when Walter left on his final trip of the season, the corn was suffering badly. The leaves were turning brown and curling inward, and the stalks were prematurely golden. While he was gone, Lisetta prayed for rain, but her heart wasn't in it. She was thinking, *Why should God send down rain specifically to the land east of Hoskins and west of Winside? Why their little community?* *The Lord's Prayer says 'Thy will be done,' not Lisetta Getzmer's will. Perhaps it is not in our best interest to have this struggle on the farm perpetuated. Perhaps God has other plans for our lives.*

The rain did not come. When Walter got back, there was no corn to pick.

"Lisetta," he said, "we have to sit down and talk about our future."

"I know it."

"We don't have any corn again this year. I feel bad that we can't give your mother her share. Thank heavens there was some oats to share, but I feel like a leech on your mother."

"I do too, Walt."

"We'll be struggling again all winter, trying to feed our animals."

"I know."

"I think we should have a farm sale – sell our equipment and our animals, and give the chickens back to your mother."

"And then what?"

"Well, with the money from the sale, we can rent a house in Hoskins, and if nothing else, I can get a job with the WPA, at least through the winter. The pay is measly, but between that and that little insurance business I bought from Mr. Rohrke, we can wait it out until hail adjusting season starts again. What do you think?"

"I don't know how Ma would feel about it."

"Have a talk with her tomorrow."

"I'm not surprised," Minnie said when Lisetta broached the subject. "You've had two years of bad luck, and I've been feeling guilty that I encouraged you to come onto the farm in times like these."

"You were only thinking of our own good, Ma."

"Well, Zettie, tell Walt that I'll buy your few hogs. I can put them in with mine in the hog barn, and Lyle might buy your cows. The equipment you'll have to sell at a farm sale."

The bad luck followed the little family of four through to their last day on the farm. Jeannine was running behind Walter as he carried out some trash to be burned. She stumbled and fell, cutting her nose. Lisetta bandaged it the best she could, but Minnie was the one to console the child.

"Come on, mein Liebchen," she said, comforting Jeannine. "Let's make some taffy."

*   *   *

By October, the Walt Getzmer family were situated in a little brown house in Hoskins, across the street from the parochial school, and just around the corner from Aunt Hannah's house. It was a five-room house: living room, dining room, kitchen, and two bedrooms. There was a tiny bathroom, too, but it had no fixtures and no indoor plumbing. There was an outhouse in the backyard, a pump outside the kitchen door, and a hand pump at the kitchen sink.

During the fall, Walter worked alongside a group of men who earned seventy-five cents a day with the Works Progress Administration, funded by the federal government. Their job was to tear down most of the deserted buildings in Hoskins: the high school, drugstore, butcher shop, and the depot. Only the old hotel was left standing.

"I hate to see those old buildings go," said Lisetta to Walter. "They carry so many memories."

"I know. It's the end of an era. When I was a little boy, Hoskins was a thriving town."

"In my mind, I can still see all of the horses and carriages lined up and down the street."

"And hear the train pulling into the depot."

"And see the ladies in their long dresses, stopping to chat in German."

"And your dad and my dad driving through the town together in a spring wagon."

"Ja, it's the end of an era."

By the time winter came, the old buildings were gone, and the WPA set the men to work shoveling snow. But the wages for this were only fifty cents a day. One evening in December, after shoveling snow all day, Walter came home exhausted.

"Walt, sit here and I'll bring you a hot cup of coffee," Lisetta said, motioning to an armchair. Walter plopped into the chair.

"Who was working today, Walt?"

"The usual bunch. And there was the usual bunch at the pool hall, not working. On my way home, one of those loafers stepped out and said, 'Working for the WPA, Walt? I wouldn't work for what they pay.' I told him that I have a wife and two little girls to feed, and I said, "At the end of the day I had fifty cents more, and you had nothing."

"Good for you, Walt. I'm sure the Almighty has better things in mind for you."

"For all four of us, darling."

In spite of Walter's exhaustion, he and Lisetta had a heart-to-heart talk after Lisetta had tucked the girls into bed for the night.

"You know what, Walt, maybe we should leave this area and head west like so many of your family and mine have done."

"Oh, Lisetta! Pull up our roots and give up the land?"

"We've tried so hard to survive here."

"But, Lisetta, the land is worth struggling for. When the pioneers came, the prairie was here. They claimed it for their own and turned it into farmland. When they died, they left it for future generations to take care of and to cherish it. Remember, you will inherit a farm from Minnie. I will have to earn mine, but I'll eventually own a piece of the land. I'm sure of it."

"You will, Walt. You're right about the future. We should stay."

THE END

The Appendix Translation of German words and phrases to English.

 Note: German vowels with umlauts have been indicated with italics instead of the usual two dots above the vowel.

Chapter 1	Schwarzsauer	sweet/sour soup
	Ach	Oh
	Danke Gott	Thank God
Chapter 2	Guten Tag	Good day
	Kaffeekuchen	coffeecake
	Was ist los?	What's the matter?
	Schweiz	Switzerland
	Schafskopf	sheep's head - a card game
	Guten Abend	Good evening
	Wie geht's?	How goes it (how are you)?
	Wollen Sie denn Schafskopf spielen?	
		Do you want to play Schafskopf?
	Jawohl!	Yes, indeed!
	Wie viele Schlafzimmer?	How many bedrooms?
	Mein Lieber Herr, nach Ihnen	My dear sir, after you
	drei tausend	three thousand
	fur zwei und zwanzig Jahre	for 22 years
	funf	five
	zu Hause	at home
	Wir haben zwei kleine H*a*user	We have two small houses
	unm*o*glich	impossible
	nicht so	not so

	mit	with
	ein hundert	one hundred
	Schon gut. Es wird dunkel	Okay, it's getting dark
	bis morgen	until tomorrow
	macht schnell	hurry up
Chapter 3	Nestkuchen	one who likes to stay in bed
	Er muss auch arbeiten	He has to work, too
	Alles schmeckt	Everything tastes good
	verboten	forbidden
	Halt dein Mund!	Shut up!
Chapter 4	dieser verdammte	this damned
	Er ist verruckt in dem Kopf	He's crazy in the head
	Ach, es macht nichts	Oh, it doesn't matter
	November der zehnte	November tenth
	Mein Lieber Knabe	My dear boy
Chapter 5, none		
Chapter 6, none		
Chapter 7	Schmootrine	a nonsense word
Chapter 8	Ich liebe Fruhling	I love spring
	Sommer, Herbst, Winter	summer, fall, winter
	Du liebst alle und alles	You love everyone and everything
	Ich weiss nicht	I don't know
	Deutschland	Germany
	Nein, ich muss gehen	No, I have to go
	Auf Wiedersehen	Goodbye, until we meet again
Chapter 9	Alles ist fertig	Everything is ready
	sehr hubsch	very pretty

	Danke schön	Thank you so much
	Schottische	a type of dance
Chapter 10, none		
Chapter 11, none		
Chapter 12	Ach, du altes Schwein	Oh, you old pig
	Alles weg	Everything is gone
Chapter 13	sprenkel ein bisschen Pfeffer	sprinkle a little pepper
	damit	with it
Chapter 14	Schlupps	clumsy one
	kleine	small
	Ach, Gott in Himmel!	Oh, God in heaven!
Chapter 15	mein Liebchen	my little loved one

The Author's Background

Fauneil was born in Hoskins, Nebraska and grew up in the Norfolk area. After graduating from the University of Nebraska, she took a study tour of Europe with the University of South Dakota. Her first teaching position in English and music was in Tucson, Arizona. While there, she earned an M.Ed. degree from the University of Arizona. After her marriage, she returned to a study of music and earned an MA degree from San Jose State University. As a pipe organist, she pursued her career in California until her husband retired, and they moved to Santa Fe, New Mexico.

Following the death of her husband in 2018, she began a career as an author. She moved to San Antonio, Texas in 2019, after publishing her first book, *I Didn't Really Know Him*. In Texas, she published *The Seeds of the Prairie* and *The Spirit of the Prairie* (title later changed to *Walter and Lisetta.)* After being financially scammed, she returned to California, where she wrote *Confused and Abused*. She currently lives in Stockton, California. Her most recent books are *The Story of Peter, Ruth, and Evan* and *Laurel's Journey with Her Guardian Angel*.